KEVIN ZRALY

WINDOWS ON THE WORLD

Wine Tasting Notebook

KEVIN ZRALY

WINDOWS ON THE WORLD

Wine Tasting Notebook

STERLING EPICURE
New York

STERLING EPICURE
New York

An Imprint of Sterling Publishing
1166 Avenue of the Americas
New York, NY 10036

New material © 2015 by Kevin Zraly

This book contains material previously published in *Kevin Zraly
Windows on the World Complete Wine Course: 30th Anniversary
Edition* © 2014 by Kevin Zraly

ISBN 978-1-4549-1783-0

Distributed in Canada by Sterling Publishing
c/o Canadian Manda Group, 664 Annette Street
Toronto, Ontario, M6S 2C8, Canada
Distributed in the United Kingdom by GMC Distribution Services
Castle Place, 166 High Street, Lewes, East Sussex, BN7 1XU, England
Distributed in Australia by Capricorn Link (Australia) Pty. Ltd.
P.O. Box 704, Windsor, NSW 2756, Australia

For information about custom editions, special sales, and premium
and corporate purchases, please contact Sterling Special Sales at
800-805-5489 or specialsales@sterlingpublishing.com.

Manufactured in Canada

2 4 6 8 10 9 7 5 3 1

www.sterlingpublishing.com

CONTENTS

"There are no standards of taste in wine, cigars, poetry, prose, etc. Each man's own taste is the standard, and a majority vote cannot decide for him or in any slightest degree affect the supremacy of his own standard."

—MARK TWAIN, 1895

AUTHOR'S NOTE

I began my wine journey as a nineteen-year-old college student and, like most students, I had a negative cash flow. I was lucky, though, to have worked weekends in a fabulous restaurant that had a small but well-selected wine list. The only way for me to learn about wine was to go to as many industry-sponsored (meaning: free) wine tastings as I could.

These usually were stand-up tastings featuring hundreds of different wines. The only way to survive them and remember the wines the next day was to take copious notes. So I created my own journal, a rating system, and collected labels for reference as I continued my wine studies. I still have those notes and labels today. Having a notebook gave me a great way to track my wine education and taste preferences over the years, and I hope that this notebook allows you to do the same. Good luck on your own wine journey, and may your glass always be half full!

—KEVIN ZRALY

GRAPES OF THE WORLD AND THEIR FLAVORS

Let's start with the three major grapes you need to know to understand white wine. More than 90 percent of all quality white wine is made from these three grapes. They are, in order from the lightest style to the fullest: Riesling, Sauvignon Blanc, and Chardonnay. Here is where they grow best:

White Grapes of the World

RIESLING: Germany; Alsace, France; New York State; Washington State

SAUVIGNON BLANC: Bordeaux, France; Loire Valley, France; New Zealand; California (Fumé Blanc)

CHARDONNAY: Burgundy, France; Champagne, France; California

World-class Rieslings, Sauvignon Blancs, and Chardonnays are also made in other countries, but in general the above regions specialize in wines made from these grapes.

MORE WELL KNOWN WHITE GRAPES AND REGIONS TO EXPLORE

GRAPES	WHERE THEY GROW BEST
Albariño	Spain
Chenin Blanc	Loire Valley, France; California
Gewürztraminer and Pinot Blanc	Alsace, France
Grüner Veltliner	Austria
Pinot Grigio/Gris	Italy; California; Oregon; Alsace, France
Sémillon	Bordeaux (Sauternes); Australia
Viognier	Rhône Valley, France; California

OTHER WHITE-GRAPE VARIETALS AND REGIONS WHERE THEY CAN BE FOUND

Assyrtiko	Greece
Furmint	Hungary
Hárslevelü	Hungary
Macabeo	Spain
Moschofilero	Greece
Olaszrizling	Hungary
Roditis	Greece
Szürkebarát	Hungary
Torrontés Riojano	Argentina
Trebbiano	Italy
Verdejo	Spain
Vidal	Canada

See page 24 for more information on where white grapes grow best.

Red Grapes of the World

On the following page is a list of what I consider the major red-wine grapes, ranked from lightest style to fullest, along with the region or country in which the grape grows best. This chart will give you an idea of the style of the wine and also a feeling for gradations of weight, color, tannin, and ageability.

Remember, there are always exceptions to the rule, just as other countries and wine regions not listed here produce world-class wine from some of the red grapes shown.

MORE WELL KNOWN RED GRAPES AND REGIONS TO EXPLORE

GRAPES	WHERE THEY GROW BEST
Barbera	Italy
Dolcetto	Italy
Cabernet Franc	Loire Valley and Bordeaux, France
Grenache/ Garnacha	Rhône Valley, France Spain
Malbec	Bordeaux and Cahors, France; Argentina

GRAPES	WHERE THEY GROW BEST
Gamay	Beaujolais, France
Pinot Noir	Burgundy, France; Champagne, France; California; Oregon
Tempranillo	Rioja, Spain
Sangiovese	Tuscany, Italy Bordeaux, France;
Merlot	Napa, California
Zinfandel	California
Cabernet Sauvignon	Bordeaux, France; Napa, California; Chile
Nebbiolo	Piedmont, Italy
Syrah/Shiraz	Rhône Valley, France; Australia; California

OTHER RED-GRAPE VARIETALS AND REGIONS WHERE THEY CAN BE FOUND

Agiorgitiko	Greece
Barbera	Italy, California
Blaufränkisch	Austria
Cariñena	Spain
Carmenère	Chile
Cinsault	Rhône Valley
Concord	United States
Kadarka	Hungary
Kékfrankos	Hungary
Monastrell	Spain

TEXTURE	TANNIN LEVEL	COLOR LEVEL	AGEABILITY
Light	Low	Lighter	Drink Young
↓	↓	↓	↓
Full-bodied	High	Deeper	Wine to Age

Petite Syrah	California
Pinot Meunier	Champagne
Portugieser	Hungary
Saint Laurent	Austria
Xinomavro	Greece

See page 26 for more information on where red grapes grow best.

GRAPE VARIETIES AND THEIR FLAVORS

GRAPE VARIETY	GRAPE FLAVORS	WINEMAKING AND AGING FLAVORS
Cabernet Sauvignon	Cassis (black currant) Blackberry Violets	Pencil shavings Toast Tobacco—dead leaf
Grenache	Cherries Raspberries Spicy	Concentrations Extraction
Merlot	Blackberries Black olive Plum	Pencil shavings Toast
Nebbiolo	Plum Raspberries Truffle Acidity	Strong tea Nutmeg Gamey
Pinot Noir	Perfumed Raspberries Red cherry Acidity	Smoky Earthy
Sangiovese	Black cherries Blackberries Violets Spice	Cedar Plum Vanilla

GRAPE VARIETY	GRAPE FLAVORS	WINEMAKING AND AGING FLAVORS
Syrah/Shiraz	Spicy Black fruits Blueberry	Toasty Vanilla Coffee
Tempranillo	Fruity Cherries	Oak (American) Tobacco
Zinfandel	Spicy Ripe berries Cherries	Savory Tar Chocolate
Chardonnay	Apple Melon Pear	Vanilla Toast Butterscotch
Riesling	Minerality Citrus Tropical fruit Acidity	Steely Green apples Petrol
Sauvignon Blanc	Tomato stalk Cut grass Grapefruit Citrus Aromatic	Coconut Smoky Vanilla

HOW TO READ A WINE LABEL

California labels tell you everything you need to know about the wine—and more. Here are some quick tips you can use when you scan the shelves at your favorite retailer. The Rudd label shown below will serve as an example.

STATE: California
COUNTY: Sonoma
VITICULTURAL AREA (AVA): Russian River Valley
VINEYARD: Bacigalupi
WINERY: Rudd

The most important piece of information on the label is the producer's name. In this case, the producer is Rudd.

This label shows that the wine is made from the Chardonnay grape. If the grape variety is on the label, a minimum of 75 percent of the wine must be derived from that grape variety.

If the wine bears a vintage date, 95 percent of the grapes must have been harvested that year.

If the wine is designated "California," then 100 percent of the grapes must have been grown in California.

If the label designates a certain federally recognized viticultural area (AVA), such as the Russian River Valley (as on our sample label), then at least 85 percent of the grapes used to make that wine must have been grown in that location.

The alcohol content is given in percentages. Usually, the higher the percentage of alcohol, the "fuller" the wine will be.

"Produced and bottled by" means that at least 75 percent of the wine was fermented by the winery named on the label.

Some wineries tell you the exact varietal content of the wine, and/or the sugar content of the grapes when they were picked, and/or the amount of residual sugar (to let you know how sweet or dry the wine is).

FREQUENTLY ASKED QUESTIONS ABOUT WINE

What is tannin, and is it desirable in wine?

Tannin is a natural preservative and one of the many components that give wine its longevity. It comes from the skins, pits, and stems of grapes. Another source of tannin is wood, such as the oak barrels in which some wines are aged or fermented. Generally, red wines have a higher level of tannin than whites because red grapes are usually left to ferment with their skins.

A word used to describe the sensation of tannins is *astringent*. Especially in young wines, tannin can be very astringent and make the wine taste bitter. Tannin is not a taste, however—it's a tactile sensation.

Tannin is also found in strong tea. What can you add to tea to make it less astringent? Milk—the fat and the proteins in milk soften the tannin. So it is with a highly tannic wine. If you take another milk byproduct, such as cheese, and have it with wine, it softens the tannin and makes the wine more appealing. Enjoy a beef entrée or one served with a cream sauce and a young, tannic red wine to experience it for yourself.

Is acidity desirable in wine?

All wine will have a certain amount of acidity. Generally, white wines have more perceived acidity than reds, though winemakers try to have a balance of fruit and acid. An overly acidic wine is also described as tart or sour. Acidity is a very important component in the aging of wines. As sugar levels increase, the perceived taste of acidity decreases.

FIVE HIGH-ACID GRAPES

Nebbiolo (red)

Sangiovese (red)

Pinot Noir (red)

Riesling (white)

Chenin Blanc (white)

What is meant by *vintage*? Why is one year considered better than another?

A vintage indicates the year the grapes were harvested, so every year is a vintage year. A vintage chart reflects the weather conditions for various years. Better weather usually results in a better rating for the vintage and therefore a higher likelihood that the wine will age well.

Does the age of the vine affect the quality of the wine?

You sometimes will see on French wine labels the term *Vieilles Vignes* ("old vines"). In California, I've tasted many Zinfandels made from vines more than seventy-five years old. Many wine tasters, including myself, believe that these old vines create a different complexity and taste than do younger vines.

In many countries, grapes from young vines will not be made into a winery's top wine. In Bordeaux, France, Château Lafite-Rothschild produces a second wine, called Carruades de Lafite-Rothschild, which is made from the vineyard's youngest vines (less than fifteen years old).

As a vine ages, especially over thirty years, it starts losing its fruit-production value. Most vines are replanted by their fiftieth birthday.

Do all wines need corks?

It is a time-honored tradition more than two centuries old to use corks to preserve wine. Most corks come from cork oak trees grown in Portugal and Spain. Most wines could be sold without using cork as a stopper. Since 90 percent of all wine is meant to be consumed within one year, a screw cap will work just as well, if not better, than a cork for most wines. Just think what this would mean to you—no need for a corkscrew, no broken corks and, most important, no more tainted wine caused by contaminated cork.

I do believe that certain wines—those with potential to age for more than five years—are much better off using cork. But also keep in mind, for those real wine collectors, that a cork's life span is approximately twenty-five to thirty years, before which you'd better drink the wine or find somebody to recork it.

Many wineries around the world use the Stelvin screw cap, especially in California (Bonny Doon, Sonoma-Cutrer, etc.), Australia, New Zealand, and Austria.

What's the difference between California and French wines, and who makes the better wines?

California and France both make great wines, but the French make the best French wines!

From production strategy to weather, each region's profile is distinct. California wines and French wines share many similarities. The greatest similarity is that both France and California grow most of the same grape varieties. They also have many differences. The biggest differences are soil, climate, and tradition.

The French regard their soil with reverence and believe that the best wines come from only the greatest soil. When grapes originally were planted in California, the soil was not one of the major factors in determining which grapes were planted where. Over recent decades, this has become a much more important aspect for the vineyard owners in California, and today winemakers refer to their best Cabernet Sauvignons as coming from a specific area or vineyard.

As far as weather goes, the temperatures in Napa and Sonoma are different from those in Burgundy and Bordeaux. The fact is, that while European vintners get gray hair over pesky problems like cold snaps and rainstorms in the growing season, Californians can virtually count on abundant sunshine and warm temperatures.

Tradition is the biggest difference between the two, and I'm not just talking about winemaking. For example, vineyard and winery practices in Europe have remained virtually unchanged for generations, and these age-old techniques—some written into law—define each region's own style. But in California, where few traditions exist, vintners are free to experiment with modern technology and create new products based on consumer demand. If you've ever had a wine called Two Buck Chuck, you know what I mean.

It is sometimes very difficult for me to sit in a tasting and compare a California Chardonnay and a French white Burgundy, since they've been making wines in Burgundy for the last 1,600 years, and the renaissance of California wines is not yet fifty years old.

I buy both French and California wines for my personal cellar, and sometimes my choice has to do totally with how I feel that day or what food I'm having: Do I want to end up in Bordeaux or the Napa Valley?

When is a wine ready to drink?

This is one of the most frequently asked questions. The answer is very simple: when all components of the wine are in balance to your particular taste.

How do you know whether a wine is good?

The definition of a good wine is one that you enjoy. I cannot emphasize this enough. Trust your own palate, and do not let others dictate taste to you!

Why do I get a headache when I drink wine?

The simple answer may be overconsumption! Seriously, though, more than 10 percent of my students are medical doctors, and none of them has been able to give me the definitive answer to this question.

Some people get headaches from white wine, others from red, but when it comes to alcohol consumption, dehydration certainly plays an important role in how you feel the next day. That's why, for every glass of wine I consume, I will have two glasses of water to keep my body hydrated.

Many factors influence the way your system metabolizes alcohol. The top three are:

1. Health
2. DNA
3. Gender

Research is leaning increasingly toward genetics as a reason for chronic headaches.

For those of you who have allergies, different levels of histamines are present in red wines; these can obviously cause discomfort and headaches. I myself have a slight allergy to red wine, and I "suffer" every day.

Many doctors have told me that food additives contribute to headaches. There is a natural compound in red wine called tyramine, which is said to dilate blood vessels. Further, combining alcohol and prescription medicines is frequently contraindicated.

Regarding gender, due to certain stomach enzymes, women absorb more alcohol into their bloodstream than men do. A doctor who advises women that one glass of wine a day is a safe limit is likely to tell men that they can drink two glasses.

What happens when I can't finish the whole bottle of wine?

This is one of the most frequently asked questions in Wine School (although I have never had this problem).

If you still have a portion of the wine left over, whether red or white, the bottle should be corked and immediately put into the refrigerator. Don't leave it out on your kitchen counter. Remember, bacteria grow in warm temperatures, and a 70°F+ kitchen will spoil wine very quickly. If refrigerated, most wines will not lose their flavor over a 48-hour period. (Some people swear that the wine even tastes better, although I'm not among them.)

Eventually, the wine will begin to oxidize. This is true of all table wines with an 8 to 14 percent alcohol content. Other wines, such as Ports and Sherries, with a higher alcohol content of 17 to 21 percent, will last longer, but I wouldn't suggest keeping them longer than two weeks.

Remember, the most harmful thing to wine is oxygen, and the less contact with oxygen, the longer the wine will last. That's why some wine collectors also use something called the Vacu-Vin, which pumps air out of the bottle. Other wine collectors spray the bottle with an inert gas such as nitrogen, which is odorless and tasteless, that preserves the wine from oxygen.

Remember, if all else fails, you'll still have a great cooking wine!

Are all wines meant to be aged?

No. It's a common misconception that all wines improve with age. In fact, more than 90 percent of all wines in the world should be consumed within one year, and less than 1 percent of the world's wines should be aged for more than five years. Wines change with age. Some get better, but most do not. The good news is that the 1 percent represents more than 350 million bottles of wine every vintage.

How long should I age my wine?

The *Wall Street Journal* recently published an article stating that most people have one or two wines that they've been saving for years for a special occasion. This is probably not a good idea!

The following are wines that will get better with age:

WHITE

California Chardonnay	2–10+ years
French White Burgundy	3–8+ years
German Riesling (Auslese, Beerenauslese, and Trockenbeerenauslese)	3–30+ years
French Sauternes	3–30+ years

RED

California/Oregon Pinot Noirs	2–5+ years
French Red Burgundy	3–8+ years
California Merlot	2–10+ years
Chianti Classico Riservas	3–10+ years
Argentine Malbec	3–15+ years
Brunello di Montalcino	3–15+ years

California Cabernet Sauvignon	3–15+ years
California Zinfandel	5–15+ years
Spanish Riojas (Gran Reservas)	5–20+ years
Barolo and Barbaresco	5–25+ years
Hermitage/Syrah	5–25+ years
Bordeaux Châteaux	5–30+ years
Vintage Ports	10–40+ years

There are always exceptions to the rule when it comes to generalizing about the aging of wine (especially considering the variations in vintages), hence the plus signs in the previous list.

There are many great wine regions that produce red wines that will age for thirty or more years. But nowhere else on Earth other than Bordeaux is there a region that produces both red and white wines that you can drink 100 years later! I have had Bordeaux wines more than a hundred years old that were still going strong. It is also not unlikely to find a great Sauternes or Port that still needs time to age after its fiftieth birthday. But the age spans represent more than 95 percent of the wines in their respective categories.

WHAT MAKES A GREAT WINE GREAT?

Varietal character
Balance of components
Complexity
Sense of place
Emotional response

What's the best bottle size for aging?

Magnum (1.5 liter)

My wine collector and winemaker friends say that their best wines will last longer and mature more slowly in a magnum (2 bottles) than in a 750 ml. One of the theories for this difference in bottle-size aging is the amount of air in the bottle (the air between the wine and the cork) versus the quantity of wine. It's also more fun to serve a magnum at a dinner party.

What's the best temperature for wine storage?

55°F

This is the temperature at which all the great wineries store and age their wine. If you have a wine collection or are planning on collecting wines, you must protect your investment. Studies have shown that the best temperature for long-term wine storage is approximately 55°F. The same studies have also shown that storing wine at 75°F ages wine twice as fast. Just as warm temperatures will prematurely age the wine, temperatures too cold can freeze the wine, pushing out the cork and immediately ending the aging process.

You can either buy a wine refrigerator or build a wine cellar with the proper air conditioning.

What's the best red wine with fish?

Pinot Noir

It's light, easy, not overpowering, usually has high acidity and low tannin, and blends nicely with all different types of food. It's a "white wine" masquerading as a red. Pinot Noir is the perfect wine for a dinner of six or eight where everyone is having something different, from fish to poultry or meat.

Other choices include Chianti Classico and Spanish Riojas (Crianza and Reserva). For barbecued or grilled fish or shrimp in the middle of the summer, I opt for chilled Beaujolais-Village or Cru.

What's the best white wine with meat?

Chardonnay

Whoever coined the phrase "white wine with fish" was probably thinking of Riesling, Pinot Grigio, and Sauvignon Blanc, since a vast majority of Chardonnays will overpower fish dishes, except possibly a tuna, salmon, or swordfish steak.

Many Chardonnays are "red wines" masquerading as whites, especially the big, oaky, high-alcohol Chardonnays from California and Australia. Usually, the more expensive the Chardonnay, the more oaky it will be. With all of its flavor, weight, and tannin, the perfect match for Chardonnay is something like a sirloin steak!

What's the best wine for chicken?

Anything

Chicken is one of the best things to have with wine because it doesn't have an overpowering flavor. It can go with almost any wine—red or white, light, medium, or full.

What's the best wine for chocolate?

Port

For me, both chocolate and Port mean the end of the meal. They are both rich, sweet, satisfying, and sometimes even decadent together.

What's the best wine for lamb?

Bordeaux or California Cabernet Sauvignon

In Bordeaux they have lamb with breakfast, lunch, and dinner! Lamb has such a strong flavor that it needs a strong wine, and the big, full-bodied Cabernet Sauvignons from California and Bordeaux blend in perfectly.

What's the best wine to have in a restaurant?

Anything under $75!

Even though I've been in the restaurant business most of my life, I think it is one of the worst places to experiment with wine tasting. Restaurants are notorious for their markup on wines, sometimes double and triple what you will pay retail. It is easy for me to choose $100+ bottles of wine. But I find it more interesting to find a $25 bottle of wine that tastes like a $50, a $50 bottle that tastes like a $100, and so on.

A few years ago, while working with Tim and Nina Zagat, I reviewed over 125 restaurant wine lists in New York City. Tim and I both agree that normally we don't spend more than $75 for a bottle of wine in a restaurant, unless someone else is paying! I was reviewing all of these wine lists to find out what the percentage was of wines under $50, under $75, and under $100. To my surprise most of these restaurants had a large percentage of affordable wines! Restaurants with high-price wines and very few wines under $75 do not get my credit card.

What's the best red wine for lunch?

Pinot Noir

Since most of us have to go back to work after lunch, the light, easy-drinking style of a Pinot Noir will not overpower your usual luncheon fare of soups, salads, and sandwiches.

What's the best white wine for lunch

Riesling

Depending upon what you are having for lunch, you could go with the low-alcohol (8 to 10 percent) German Riesling Kabinett—its slight residual sugar will blend in nicely, especially with salads.

For those who prefer a drier style, a French Alsace, Washington State, Australia, or Finger Lakes Riesling are great choices.

What's the best wine for Thanksgiving?

This is one of the most asked wine and food questions that I get that I don't have a definitive answer for. The problem with Thanksgiving is that it's not just the turkey, but everything

else that is served with it—sweet potatoes,
cranberries, butternut squash, stuffing—that can
create havoc with wine.

This is also the big family holiday in the
United States, and do you really want to share
your best wines with your relatives? I suggest
that you try "user friendly" wines: easy-
drinking, inexpensive wines from reliable
producers. Check out the lists on pages 31–52
for more specific wines.

We have one tradition at our Thanksgiving
family dinner, which is to serve an
Amontillado Sherry and/or a Tawny Port after
the turkey with a selection of nuts and fruits.

What's the best place on Earth for Riesling

Germany

Runners-up: Alsace, France, and the Finger Lakes District, New York State

Many professionals and wine connoisseurs
believe that the best white wine in the world is
Riesling. It is definitely one of the best wines
with food, especially with lighter-style fish such
as sole and flounder.

Some 95 percent of all Alsace Rieslings are
dry. In the Finger Lakes, they produce dry,
semidry, and sweet Rieslings.

The diversity of style of the German wines—
some dry, off-dry, semisweet, and very sweet—
is the reason I would rank German Rieslings as
the best in the world.

What's the best place on Earth for Sauvignon Blanc?

Loire Valley, France

Runners-up: New Zealand and California

The Sauvignon Blanc produced in the Loire Valley is best known by its regional names, Sancerre and Pouilly-Fumé. The best of the New Zealand and California Sauvignon Blancs are sold under the producer's name.

The stylistic differences between the Sauvignon Blancs of the Loire Valley and New Zealand are striking. While both Sauvignon Blancs are light to medium in body with high acidity, and work well with fish and poultry, the New Zealand Sauvignon Blancs have what some would call a very tropical aroma, which you either like or don't. I like it! After Chardonnay, Sauvignon Blanc is the second-highest-quality white grape grown in California. In my opinion, the best Sauvignon Blancs are from cooler climates, have no oak, and are lower in alcohol content.

What's the best place on Earth for Chardonnay?

Burgundy, France

Runner-up: California

As much as I like the best producers of California Chardonnay, the elegance and balance of fruit and acidity of a white Burgundy wine is unmatched in the world. From the non-oak-aged Chablis and the barrel-fermented and barrel-aged Montrachets to the light, easy-drinking Mâcons and the world famous Pouilly-Fuissé, there is a style and a price for everyone.

As with Sauvignon Blanc, the best Chardonnays of California are coming from the cooler climates such as Carneros and Santa Barbara. I am not a fan of high-alcohol, overly oaked Chardonnays.

What's the best place on Earth for Pinot Noir?

Burgundy, France

Runners-up: Oregon and California

Burgundy is a region with deep history and tradition. Vines have been planted there for over a thousand years, and the sensuous Pinot Noir is the only red grape allowed (except for Beaujolais).

The only problem with a great Pinot Noir from Burgundy is its price tag and availability. Oregon makes the best Pinot Noirs in the United States, and many refer to the wines of Oregon as the "Burgundy of the United States" since their emphasis is on Chardonnay and Pinot Noir. In California, the best Pinot Noirs are also grown in the cooler climates.

What's the best place on Earth for Merlot?

Bordeaux, France (Saint-Émilion, Pomerol)

Runner-up: California

The number-one red grape planted in Bordeaux is Merlot.

The great châteaux of Saint-Émilion and Pomerol produce wines made primarily of the Merlot grape. The major difference between the two is the price and availability of each wine region. There are only 1,986 acres in Pomerol, but Saint-Émilion has over 23,062 acres of vines in production. For my money, I'd go with Saint-Émilion.

What's the best place on Earth for Cabernet Sauvignon?

Bordeaux, France (Médoc)

Runner-up: California

Best Value: Chile

In my opinion, the greatest wines in the world are the châteaux of Bordeaux.

The primary red grape of the Médoc is Cabernet Sauvignon. With some 7,000 châteaux, there's plenty of wine to choose from at all different price points.

The best Cabernet Sauvignon from California comes from the North Coast counties, especially Napa and Sonoma. The Napa Cabernets usually have more intensity of fruit and body and the Cabernets from Sonoma generally are softer and more elegant.

The price of an acre of vineyard land in Chile is so far below that of Napa Valley and Bordeaux, and you will find tremendous quality and value.

What's the best wineglass?

Riedel

The Riedel family of Austrian glassmakers has strived for over thirty years to elevate wine drinking to a new level with specially designed varietal glassware. They have designed glasses to accentuate the best components of each grape variety, their opinion being that a Cabernet Sauvignon/Bordeaux glass should be different from a Pinot Noir/Burgundy glass.

Riedel glasses comes in many different styles. There are wineglasses for special occasions and everyday wine use. The top of the line is the handcrafted Sommelier series. Next comes the moderate-price collection with the Vinum. For those of you who do not want to spend a tremendous amount of money on glassware, their least expensive series in the competitive line is the Ouverture.

What are the best wine regions for a vacation?

Napa Valley, California

Tuscany, Italy

Bordeaux, France

A great vacation for me is great wine, fabulous restaurants, perfect climate, proximity to the ocean, beautiful scenery (am I asking too much yet?), and nice people! These three wine regions fulfill my needs.

What's the best wine lie?

That all wines get better with age

Think of all of the wines that you used to drink in high school and college. Now think about how much you used to pay for those wines! I'm sure they didn't stay around very long! Which is exactly the way it should be.

The reality is that 90 percent of all wines are meant to be consumed within one year and that another 9 percent of wines should not see more than five years of age. Which leaves us with less than 1 percent of wines made in the world today that can age over five years.

What's the best wine myth?

That everyone tastes wine alike

No one tastes wine or anything else alike. Sense of taste and smell are like your own fingerprint or a snowflake—no two are the same. The average person has 3,000 to 10,000 taste buds. Since it is very difficult to measure how many taste buds one has, I can trust only my own judgment and no one else's. The sense of smell is even more important than the sense of taste. (We all know this from when we have a cold.) You can taste only five things in life, but the average person can smell over 2,000 smells, and there are some 200 smells in wine. Other factors include age, medical injuries (deviated septum), and side effects from prescription medicine.

What are the most important books for your wine library?

The following is a list of general books I consider required reading if you want to delve further into this fascinating subject:

Hugh Johnson's Modern Encyclopedia of Wine

World Atlas of Wine, Hugh Johnson and Jancis Robinson

Sotheby's Wine Encyclopedia, Tom Stevenson

Oxford Companion to Wine, Jancis Robinson

The Wine Bible, Karen MacNeil

Wine for Dummies, Ed McCarthy and
   Mary Ewing-Mulligan

Oz Clarke's New Essential Wine Book

Oz Clarke's New Encyclopedia of Wine

Oz Clarke's Wine Atlas

Great Wine Made Simple, Andrea Robinson

Since the above volumes are sometimes encyclopedic in nature, I always carry with me one of these three pocket guides to wine:

Hugh Johnson's Pocket Wine Book

Oz Clarke's Pocket Wine Book

What's the best place to check the right price for a bottle of wine?

wine-searcher.com

BEST VALUE WINES:
$30 AND UNDER

Today there are hundreds of wines priced under $30 that are equal in quality to wines that I have tasted that cost over $100. Bottom line: This is one of the best times ever for buying a very good bottle of wine at a reasonable price. There are many great wine values in the world that I would have included in this chapter, but many are not available in all markets and therefore are not listed. Most wines in this section are $30 or under, but I have also added some that I think are great values, even if they are over $30.

France

Although France sometimes has a reputation for very expensive wines (great Châteaux of Bordeaux, Domaines of Burgundy, etc.) there always have been great values made in France. From Alsace: Rieslings, Pinot Blancs, and Pinot Gris; from the Loire Valley:

Muscadet, Sancerre, and Pouilly-Fumé; from Burgundy: Beaujolais, Mâcons, Chablis, and Bourgogne Blanc and Rouge; from the Rhône Valley: Côtes du Rhône and Crozes-Hermitage; from Bordeaux: Petit Château and Cru Bourgeois; and the wines from Provence, Languedoc, and Roussillon areas. Here are some of my favorite French producers and their value wines:

RED

"A" d'Aussières Rouge Corbières

Baron de Brane

Brunier Le Pigeoulet Rouge VDP Vaucluse

Brunier "Megaphone" Ventoux Rouge

Chapelle-St-Arnoux Châteauneuf-du-Pape Vieilles Vignes

Château Bel Air

Château Cabrières Côtes du Rhône

Château Cap de Faugeres

Château Caronne-Sainte-Gemme

Château Chantegrive

Château de Maison Neuve

Château de Mercey Mercurey Rouge

Château d'Escurac "Pepin"

Château de Trignon Gigondas

Château de Villambis

Château Greysac

Château Haut du Peyrat

Château Labat

Château La Cardonne

Château Larose-Trintaudon

Château Le Bonnat

Château Le Sartre

Château Malmaison

Château Malromè

Château Maris La Touge Syrah

Château Peyrabon

Château Pey La Tour Reserve du Château

Château Puy-Blanquet

Château Puynard

Château Saint Julian

Château Segondignac

Château Thébot

Château Tour Leognan

Cheval Noir

Clos Siguier Cahors

Côte-de-Nuits-Village, Joseph Drouhin

Croix Mouton

Cuvée Daniel Côtes de Castillon

Domaine André Brunel Côtes-du-Rhône Cuvée Sommelongue

Domaine Bouchard Pinot Noir

Domaine d'Andezon Côtes-du-Rhône

Domaine de la Coume du Roy Côtes du Roussillon-Villages "Le Desir"

Domaine de Lagrézette Cahors

Domaine de'Obrieu Côtes du Rhône Villages "Cuvée les Antonins"

Domaine de Villemajou "Boutenac"

Domaine Michel Poinard Crozes-Hermitage

Domaine Roches Neuves Saumur-Champigny

Georges Duboeuf Beaujolais-Villages

Georges Duboeuf Morgon "Cave Jean-Ernest Descombes"

Gérard Bertrand Domaine de L'Aigle Pinot Noir

Gérard Bertrand Grand Terroir Tautavel

Gilles Ferran "Les Antimagnes"

Guigal Côtes du Rhône

Jaboulet Côtes du Rhône Parallèle 45

Jaboulet Crozes-Hermitage Les Jalets

Jean-Maurice Raffault Chinon

Joseph Drouhin Côte de Beaune-Villages

J. Vidal-Fleury Côtes du Rhône

La Baronne Rouge "Montagne d'Alaric"

Lafite Réserve Spéciale

Laplace Madiran

La Vieille Ferme Côtes du Ventoux

Le Medoc de Cos

Louis Jadot Château des Jacques Moulin-à-Vent

Maison Champy Pinot Noir Signature

M. Chapoutier Bila-Haut Côtes de Rousillon Villages

Marc Rougeot Bourgogne Rouge "Les Lameroses"

Marjosse Reserve du Château

Mas de Gourgonnier Les Baux de Provence Rouge

Michel Poinard Crozes Hermitage

Montirius Gigondas Terres des Aînés

Nicolas Thienpont Selection Saint-Emilion Grand Cru

Perrin & Fils Côtes du Rhône

Rene Lequin-Colin Santenay "Vieilles Vignes"

Thiery Germain Saumur-Champigny

Villa Ponciago Fleurie La Réserve Beaujolais

WHITE

Ballot-Millot et Fils Bourgogne Chardonnay

Bertranon Bordeaux Blanc

Bouzeron Domaine Gagey

Cairanne, Domaine les Hautes Cances

Château Bonnet Blanc

Château de Maligny Petit Chablis

Château de Mercey Mercurey Blanc

Château de Rully Blanc "La Pucelle"

Château de Sancerre

Château du Mayne Blanc

Château du Trignon Côtes du Rhône Blanc

Château Fuissé

Château Graville-Lacoste Blanc

Château Loumelat

Château Martinon Blanc

Clarendelle

Claude Lafond Reuilly

Domaine de Montcy Cheverny

Domaine Delaye Saint-Véran "Les Pierres Grises"

Domaine des Baumard Savenniéres

Domaine Jean Chartron Bourgogne Aligoté

Domaine Mardon Quincy "Très Vieilles Vignes"

Domaine Paul Pillot Bourgogne Chardonnay

Domaine Saint Barbe Macon Clesse "Les Tilles"

Faiveley Bourgogne Blanc

Francis Blanchet Pouilly Fumé "Cuvée Silice"

Georges Duboeuf Pouilly-Fuissé

Helfrich Riesling

Hugel & Fils Gentil

Hugel & Fils Riesling

Hugel Pinot Gris

J.J. Vincent Pouilly-Fuissé "Marie Antoinette"

Jeanguillon Blanc

Jonathon Pabiot Pouilly Fumé

Laroche Petit Chablis

Louis Jadot Saint-Véran

Louis Latour Montagny

Louis Latour Pouilly-Vinzelles

Maison Bleue Chardonnay

Marjosse Blanc Reserve du Château

Mas Karolina Côtes Catalanes Blanc

Michel Bailly Pouilly Fumé

Olivier Leflaive Saint-Aubin

Pascal Jolivet Attitude

Pascal Jolivet Sancerre

Robert Klingenfus Pinot Blanc

Sauvion Pouilly-Fumé Les Ombelles

Sauvion Sancerre, "Les Fondettes"

Simonnet-Febvre Chablis

Thierry Germain Saumur Blanc Cuvée "Soliterre"

Thierry Pillot Santenay Blanc "Clos Genet"

Trimbach Gewurztraminer

Trimbach Riesling

William Fèvre Chablis

Willm Cuvèe Emile Willm Riesling Rèserve

Zind Humbrecht Pinot Blanc

ROSÉ

Château Miraval Côtes de Provence Rosé "Pink Floyd"

Italy

Italy is now making its best wines ever! And great values come from all over. From Tuscany: Chianti Classico Riserva, Rosso di Montalcino, and Rossi di Montepulciano; from Piedmont: Barbaras and Dolcetto; from Veneto: Valpolicella, Soave, and the sparkling wine Prosecco; and from Abruzzi:

Montelpulciano d'Abruzzo; from northern Italy the Pinot Grigios and Pinot Biancos; and from Sicily, the Nero d'Avola. Here are some of my favorite Italian producers and their value wines:

RED

Aldo Rainoldi Nebbiolo

Aleramo Barbera

Allegrini Palazzo della Torre

Allegrini Valpolicella Classico

Antinori Badia a Passignano Chianti Classico

Altesino Rosso di Altesino

Antinori Santa Cristina Sangiovese

Antinori Tormaresca Trentangeli

Baglia di Pianetto "Ramione"

Braida Barbera d'Asti "Montebruna"

Bruno Giacosa Barbera d'Alba

Cantina del Taburno Aglianico Fidelis

Caruso e Minini I Sciani Sachia

Casal Thaulero Montepulciano d'Abruzzo

Cascata Monticello Dolcetto d'Asti

Castellare di Castellina Chianti Classico

Castello Banfi Toscana Centine

Castello Monaci Liante Salice Salentino

Col d'Orcia Rosso di Montalcino

Di Majo Norante Sangiovese Terre degli Osci

Einaudi Dolcetto di Dogliani

Fattoria di Felsina Chianti Classico Riserva

Francesco Rinaldi Dolcetto d'Alba

Guado al Tasso-Antinori Il Bruciato

La Mozza Morellino di Scansano "I Perazzi"

Le Rote Vernaccia di San Gimignano

Librandi Ciro Riserva "Duca San Felice"

Lungarotti Rubesco

Manzone Nebbiolo Langhe "Crutin"

Marchesi de' Frescobaldi Chianti Rúfina

Marchesi di Barolo Barbera d'Alba

Masi "Campofiorin"

Melini Chianti Classico Riserva "La Selvanella"

Michele Chiarlo Barbera d'Asti

Mocali Rosso di Montalcino

Monchiero Carbone Barbera d'Alba

Morgante Nero d'Avola

Montesotto Chianti Classico

Podere Ciona "Montegrossoli"

Poggio al Casone La Cattura

Poggio al Tesoro Mediterra

Poggio il Castellare Rosso di Montalcino

Principe Corsini Chianti Classico "Le Corti"

Regaleali (Tasca d'Almerita) Rosso

Ruffino Chianti Classico "Riserva Ducale" (Tan label)

Ruffino "Modus"

Sandrone Nebbiolo d'Alba Valmaggiore

San Polo "Rubio"

Silvio Nardi Rosso di Montalcino

Taurino Salice Salentino

Tenuta dell'Ornellaia Le Volte

Tenuta di Arceno Arcanum Il Fauno

Tolaini "Valdisanti"

Tormaresca "Torcicoda"

Travaglini Gattinara

Valle Reale Montepulciano d'Abruzzo

Zaccagnini Montepulciano d'Abruzzo Riserva

Zenato Valpolicella

Zeni Amarone della Valpolocella

WHITE

Abbazia di Novacella Kerner

Alois Lageder Pinot Bianco

Alois Lageder Pinot Grigio

Anselmi Soave

Antinori Chardonnay della Sala Bramito del Cervo

Antinori Vermentino Guado al Tasso

Bolla Soave Classico

Bollini Trentino Pinot Grigio

Boscaini Pinot Grigio

Botromagno Gravina Bianco

Cantina Andriano Pinot Bianco

Caruso e Minini Terre di Giumara Inzolia

Ceretto "Blange" Langhe Arneis

Clelia Romano Fiano di Avellino "Colli di Lapio"

Coppo Gavi "La Rocca"

Eugenio Collavini Pinot Grigio "Canlungo"

Jermann Pinot Grigio

Kellerei Cantina Terlan Pinot Bianco

La Carraia Orvieto Classico

Le Rote Vernaccia di San Gimignano

Maculan "Pino & Toi"

Malabaila Roero Arneis

Marchetti Verdicchio dei Castelli di Jesi Classico

Marco Felluga Collio Pinot Grigio

Mastroberardino Falanghina

Paolo Scavino Bianco

Peter Zemmer Pinot Grigio

Pieropan Soave

Pighin Pinot Grigio

Sergio Mottura Grechetto "Poggio della Costa"

Sergio Mottura Orvieto

Soave Classico Pra

Terenzuola Vermentino Colli di Luni

Teruzzi & Puthod "Terre di Tufi"

Terredora Greco di Tufo (Loggia della Serra)

ROSÉ

Antinori Guado al Tasso Scalabrone Rosato

PROSECCO

Adami

Bortolomiol

La Tordera

Le Colture

Zardetto

Spain

From the time I started studying wine forty years ago, the wines of Rioja have always represented great value, especially their Crianzas and Reservas. Now the Tempranillo grape also shines in Ribera del Duero as does the Garnacha in Priorat. From Rías Baixas, we have Albariños and from Penedès we have the great Cavas (sparkling). Here are some of my favorite Spanish producers and their value wines:

RED

Alvaro Palacios Camins del Priorat

Algueira Ribiera Sacra

Antidoto Ribera del Duero Cepas Viejas

Bernabeleva Camino de Navaherreros

Baron de Ley Reserva

Beronia Rioja Reserva

Bodega Numanthia Termes

Bodegas Beronia Reserva

Bodegas Emilio Moro "Emilio Moro"

Bodegas La Cartuja Priorat

Bodegas Lan Rioja Crianza

Bodegas Leda Mas de Leda

Bodegas Marañones 30 Mil Maravedies

Bodegas Montecillo Crianza or Reserva

Bodegas Muga Reserva

Bodegas Ontañón Crianza

Campo Viejo Reserva

Clos Galena Galena

Condado de Haza Ribera del Duero

Conde de Valdemar Crianza

CUNE Rioja Crianza "Viña Real"

Descendientes de José Palacios Bierzo Pétalos

Dinastía Vivanco Selección de Familia

El Coto Crianza and Reserva

Ermita San Felices Reserva Rioja Alta

Finca Torremilanos Ribera del Duero

Joan d'Anguera Montsant Garnatxa

Marqués de Cáceres Crianza or Reserva

Marqués de Riscal Proximo Rioja

Onix Priorat

Ontañón Crianza or Reserva

Pago dee Valdoneje Bierzo

Pesquera Tinto Crianza

Rotllan Torra Priorat Crianza

Scala Dei Priorat "Negre"

Senorio de Barahonda "Carro" Tinto

Torres Gran Coronas Reserva

Urbina Rioja Gran Reserva

WHITE

Albariño Don Olegario

Bodegas Ostatu Blanco

Burgáns Albariño Rías Baixas

Castro Brey Albariño "Sin Palabras"

Condes de Albarei "Condes Do Ferreiro Albariño de Albarei"

Legaris Verdejo Rueda

Licia Galicia Albariño

Martin Codax Albarino

Pazo de Senorans Albarino

Terras Guada Albarino "O Rosal"

CAVA

Codorníu Brut Classico

Cristalino Brut

Freixenet

Segura Viudas

Argentina

Although the reputation of Argentina is made around the region of Mendoza and the Malbec grape, there are other grapes such as Bonarda, Cabernet Sauvignon, and Chardonnay that are great values.

Here are some of my favorite Argentinean producers and their value wines:

RED

Achaval-Ferrer Malbec

Alamos Malbec

Alta Vista Malbec Grand Reserva

Bodegas Esmeralda Malbec

Bodega Norton Malbec

Bodegas Renacer "Enamore"

Bodegas Weinert Carrascal

Catena Malbec

Catena Zapata Cabernet Sauvignon

Clos de los Siete Malbec

Cuvelier Los Andes "Coleccion"

Domaine Jean Bousquet Malbec

Kaiken Cabernet Sauvignon Ultra

Michel Torino Torrontes "Don David"

Miguel Mendoza Malbec Reserva

Perdriel Malbec

Salentein Malbec

Susana Balboa Malbec

Susana Balboa Cabernet Sauvignon

Terrazas Malbec Reserva

Tikal Patriota

Trapiche Oak Cask Malbec

Valentin Bianchi Malbec

WHITE

Alamos Chardonnay

Alta Vista Torrontes Premium

Bodegas Diamandes de Uco Chardonnay

Catena Chardonnay

Michel Torino Torrontés Don David Reserve

Chile

In my Wine School and when on the lecture circuit, I always say that the best value in the world for Cabernet Sauvignon is the country of Chile. Merlot, Carmenère, and Sauvignon Blanc are also other grapes to look for. Here are some of my favorite Chilean producers and their value wines:

RED

Arboldeda Carmenère

Caliterra Cabernet Sauvignon or Merlot

Carmen Carmenère

Casa Lapostolle "Cuvée Alexandre" Merlot

Concha y Toro Puente Alto Cabernet

Cousiño-Macul Antiguas Reserva

Cono Sur 20 Barrels Cabernet

Errazuriz Cabernet Sauvignon

Los Vascos Reserve Cabernet

Montes Alpha Merlot Apalta Vineyard

Montes Cabernet Sauvignon

Santa Carolina Cabernet Sauvignon

Veramonte Primus "The Blend"

Veranda Pinot Noir Ritua

Viña Aquitania Lazuli Cabernet

WHITE

Casa Lapostolle Cuvee Alexander Chardonnay

Casa Lapostolle Cuvee Alexander Valley Sauvignon Blanc

Cono Sur "Bicycle Series" Viognier

Veramonte Sauvignon Blanc

Vina Aquitania "Sol del Sol" Chardonnay "Traiguen" 2008

Australia

Thirty years ago Australia took the world by storm with great wines at great prices, and that is still true today. The most famous red grape, Shiraz, is often blended with the classic Cabernet Sauvignon grape. But there are so many other wine regions throughout this big country that it is easy to find great Cabernet Sauvignons, Chardonnays, and Sauvignon Blancs that are sold at unbelievable prices. Here are some of my favorite Australian producers and their value wines:

RED

Alice White Cabernet Sauvignon

Banrock Station Shiraz

Black Opal Cabernet Sauvignon or Shiraz

Chapel Hill Grenache "Bushvine"

Chapel Hill Shiraz "Parson's Nose"

D'Arenberg "The Footbolt" Shiraz

D'Arenberg "The Stump Jump" Red

Jacob's Creek Shiraz Cabernet

Jacob's Creek Cabernet Sauvignon

Jim Barry "The Cover Drive" Cabernet

Jim Barry Shiraz, "The Lodge Hill"

Kilikanoon "Killerman's Run" Shiraz

Langmeil Winery "Three Gardens" Shiraz/Grenache/Mourvedre

Lindeman's Shiraz Bin 50

Marquis Philips Sarah's Blend

McWilliam's Shiraz

Mollydooker "The Boxer" Shiraz

Penfolds "Bin 28 Kalimna" Shiraz

Peter Lehmann Barossa Shiraz

Rosemount Estate Shiraz Cabernet (Diamond Label)

Salomon Estate "Finnis River" Shiraz

Schild Shiraz

Taltarni T Series Shiraz

Two Hands Shiraz "Gnarly Dudes"

Yalumba Y Series Shiraz Viognier

Yangarra Shiraz Single Vineyard

WHITE

Banrock Station Chardonnay

Bogle Sauvignon Blanc

Cape Mentelle Sauvignon Blanc-Semillon

Grant Burge Chardonnay

Heggies Vineyard Chardonnay

Lindeman's Chardonnay Bin 65

Matua Valley Sauvignon Blanc

Oxford Landing Sauvignon Blanc

Pewsey Vale Dry Riesling

Rolf Binder Riesling "Highness"

Rosemount Estate Chardonnay

Saint Clair "Pioneer Block 3" Sauvignon Blanc

Saint Hallett "Poacher's Blend" White

Trevor Jones Virgin Chardonnay

Yalumba Y Series Unwooded Chardonnay

New Zealand

The two most important grapes of New Zealand are the Sauvignon Blanc for whites and Pinot Noir for reds. Its Sauvignon Blancs have become famous throughout the world with their "tropical" aromas and taste with a citrus finish. Even though the reputation of New Zealand is based on Sauvignon Blanc, it has now entered the Pinot Noir arena for quality wines. Here are some of my favorite New Zealand producers and their value wines:

RED

Babich Pinot Noir

Brancott Estate Pinot Noir Reserve

Coopers Creek Pinot Noir

Crown Range Pinot Noir

Kim Crawford Pinot Noir

Man O' War Syrah

Mt. Beautiful Pinot Noir Cheviot Hills

Mt. Difficulty Pinot Noir

Neudorf Vineyards Pinot Noir "Tom's Block" (Nelson)

Oyster Bay Pinot Noir

Peregrine Pinot Noir

Saint Clair Pinot Noir "Vicar's Choice"

Salomon & Andrew Pinot Noir

Stoneleigh Pinot Noir

Te Awa Syrah

The Crossings Pinot Noir

Yealands Pinot Noir

WHITE

Ata Rangi Sauvignon Blanc

Babich Sauvignon Blanc

Babich Unwooded Chardonnay

Brancott Estate Sauvignon Blanc

Cloudy Bay "Te Koko"

Coopers Creek Sauvignon Blanc

Cru Vin Dogs "Greyhound" Sauvignon Blanc

Giesen Sauvignon Blanc

Glazebrook Sauvignon Blanc

Isabel Estate Sauvignon Blanc

Kim Crawford Sauvignon Blanc

Kumeu River Village Chardonnay

Man O' War Sauvignon Blanc

Mohua Pinot Gris

Mohua Sauvignon Blanc

Mount Nelson Sauvignon Blanc

Mt. Difficulty Pinot Gris

Neudorf Chardonnay

Neudorf Sauvignon Blanc

Nobilo Sauvignon Blanc

Oyster Bay Sauvignon Blanc

Pegasus Bay Chardonnay

Peregrine Pinot Gris

Saint Clair Sauvignon Blanc

Salomon & Andrew
Sauvignon Blanc

Seresin Sauvignon Blanc

Stoneleigh Chardonnay

Stoneleigh Sauvignon Blanc

Te Awa Chardonnay

Te Mata "Woodthorpe"

Villa Maria "Cellar Selection"
Sauvignon Blanc

South Africa

The diversity of South African wines, from Chenin
Blanc and Sauvignon Blanc to Cabernet Sauvignon
and Pinotage, offers a lot of different choices at
great value. Here are some of my favorite South
African producers and their value wines:

RED

Boekenhoutskloof "Chocolate
Block" Meritage

Doolhof Dark Lady of the
Labyrinth Pinotage

Jardin Syrah

Kanonkop Pinotage

Mount Rozier "Myrtle Grove"
Cabernet Sauvignon

Mulderbosch Faithful Hound

Kanonkop Kadette Red

Rupert & Rothschild
Classique

Rustenberg 1682 Red Blend

Thelema Cabernet Sauvignon

WHITE

Boschendal Chardonnay

Ken Forrester Sauvignon
Blanc

Thelema Sauvignon Blanc

Tokara Chardonnay Reserve
Collection

United States

I have tasted great value wines from states such as North Carolina, Pennsylvania, Virginia, New York, and many others. Unfortunately most of these wines are available only locally. California represents the major share of the U.S. market (90 percent) with great Sauvignon Blancs and Chardonnays for the whites and Cabernet Sauvignon, Merlot, Pinot Noir, Zinfandel, and Syrah for the reds. Washington State, the second largest producer in the United States, makes very good value Sauvignon Blancs, Merlots, Chardonnays, and Cabernet Sauvignons. And, yes, there are some Pinot Noirs and Chardonnays from Oregon that can be purchased at reasonable prices. Here are some of my favorite American producers and their value wines:

CABERNET SAUVIGNON

Andrew Will	Dry Creek
Atalon	Elements by Artesa
Beaulieu	Ex Libris
B. R. Cohn Silver label	Folie a Deux
Beringer Knights Valley	Forest Glen
Broadside "Margarita Vineyard"	Freemark Abbey
	Frog's Leap
Chappellet Mountain "Cuvee Cervantes" Meritage	Gallo of Sonoma
	Geyser Peak Reserve
Chateau Sainte Michelle "Indian Wells"	Hess Select

Joel Gott

Laurel Glen Quintana

Louis M. Martini

McManis

Mt. Veeder Winery

Rodney Strong

Rutherford Vintners

Saint Francis

Sean Minor

Sebastiani

Seven Hills

Silver Palm

Stag's Leap Wine Cellars "Hands of Time"

The Calling "Rio Lago Vineyard"

Trefethen Eshcol

CHARDONNAY

Acacia

Argyle

Arrowood Grand Archer

Benziger

Bergström "Old Stones"

Beringer

Calera Central Coast

Cambria "Katherine's Vineyard"

Channing Daughters "Scuttlehole"

Chateau Saint Jean

Chateau Sainte Michelle

Clos Pegase Mitsuko's Vineyard

Columbia Crest Sémillon-Chardonnay

Covey Run

Cuvée Daniel (Au Bon Climat)

Estancia

Fetzer Vineyard Valley Oaks

Francis Ford Coppola "Director's Cut"

Heitz Cellars

Hess Select

Hogue Columbia Valley

Joel Gott

Kendall-Jackson Grand Reserve

Landmark "Overlook"

Merryvale Starmont

Mer Soleil "Silver" (unoaked)

Morgan

Rutherford Ranch

Simi

Truchard

MERLOT

Beaulieu Coastal

Benziger

Charles Krug

Chateau Sainte Michelle "Canoe Ridge"

Clos du Bois Reserve

Columbia Crest

Ferrari-Carano

Fetzer Vineyard Valley Oaks

Forest Glen

Frei Brothers

Frog's Leap

Hogue

Kendall Jackson

Markham

Miner Family "Stage Coach"

Napa Ridge

Robert Mondavi

Saint Francis

Seven Hills

Souverain

Swanson

Waterbrook

Wolffer Estate

PINOT NOIR

Acacia Carneros

Acrobat

Argyle

Artesa

A to Z Wineworks

Au Bon Climat

Au Bon Climat "La Bauge"

Benton-Lane

Buena Vista

Byron

Calera

Cambria Julia's Vineyard

Cartlidge & Browne

Castle Rock

Chapter 24 "Two Messengers"

Cloudline

Cooper Mountain

Foley Pinot Noir

Francis Ford Coppola "Director's Cut"

Garnet

Loring

Pinot Noir "Sharecropper"

Ponzi "Tavola"

Rex Hill

Siduri

Vista Verde Vineyard

Wild Horse

Wyatt

Willamette Valley Vineyards

PINOT BLANC/PINOT GRIS

Cristom Vineyard

Elk Cove Vineyards

High Hook Vineyards

King Estate "Signature Collection"

La Crema

Ponzi

RIESLING

Boundary Breaks "Ovid Line North"

Chateau Sainte Michelle "Eroica"

Dr. Konstantin Frank

Hermann J. Wiemer

SAUVIGNON BLANC

Beaulieu Coastal

Beringer

Buena Vista

Chateau Montelena

Chateau Saint Jean

Covey Run Fumé Blanc

Ferrari-Carano Fumé Blanc

Frog's Leap

Geyser Peak

Girard

Grgich Hills Fumé Blanc

Groth

Hall Winery Sauvignon Blanc

Hogue Fumé Blanc

Honig

Joel Gott

Kendall-Jackson Vintner's Reserve

Kenwood

Mason

Matanzas Creek

Provenance Sauvignon Blanc

Rodney Strong

Sbragia Family

Silverado

SYRAH/SHIRAZ

Bonny Doon "Le Cigare Volant"

Cline

De Martino

Fess Parker

Forest Glen

Justin

Qupe Bien Nacido Vineyard

Red Lava Vineyards

Zaca Mesa

ZINFANDEL

Alexander Valley "Sin Zin"

Bogle

Cline

Joel Gott

Ravenswood "Belloni"

Ravenswood Old Vine Lodi

Seghesio Sonoma

Saint Francis Old Vines

Germany

The great value white wines of Germany are found in the Kabinett and Spätlese styles. Here are some of my favorite German producers and their value wines:

WHITE

Josef Leitz Rüdesheimer Klosterlay Riesling Kabinett

Kerpen Wehlener Sonnenuhr Kabinett

Kurt Darting Dürkheimer Hochbenn Riesling Kabinett

Leitz "Dragonstone" Riesling

Meulenhof Wehlenuhr Sonnenuhr Riesling Spätlese

Saint Urbans-Hof Riesling Kabinett

Schloss Vollrads Riesling Kabinett

Selbach-Oster Zeltinger
Sonnenuhr Riesling Kabinett

Selbach Piesporter
Michelsberg Riesling
Spatlese

Weingut Max Richter
Mülheimer Sonnelay
Riesling Kabinett

Austria

The two major white grapes of Austria are Grüner
Veltliner and Riesling, perfect wines to serve
with all kinds of foods, easy to drink, and readily
available. Here are some of my favorite Austrian
producers and their value wines:

WHITE

Albert Neumeister Morillon
Steirsche Klassik

Alois Kracher Pinot Gris
Trocken

Brundlmayer Grüner Veltliner
Kamptaler Terrassen

Forstreiter "Grand Reserve"
Grüner Veltliner

Franz Etz Grüner Veltliner
(Liter)

Hirsch "Veltliner #1"

Hirsch Grüner Veltliner
Heiligenstein

Knoll Grüner Veltliner
Federspiel Trocken Wachau
Loibner

Nigl Grüner Veltliner
Kremser Freiheit

Salomon Grüner Veltliner

Salomon Riesling
Steinterrassen

Schloss Gobelsburg

Walter Glatzer Grüner
Veltliner "Dornenvogel"

RED

Glatzer Zweigelt

Sepp Moser Sepp Zweigelt

TASTING WINE

How Do We Taste?

Like smell, taste belongs to our chemical sensing system. Taste is detected by special structures called taste buds, and we have, on average, between 3,000 and 10,000 of them, mainly on the tongue but with a few at the back of the throat and on the palate. Taste buds are the only sensory cells that are replaced regularly throughout a person's lifetime, with total regeneration taking place approximately every ten days. Scientists are examining this phenomenon, hoping that they will discover ways to replicate the process, inducing regeneration in damaged sensory and nerve cells.

Clustered within each taste bud are gustatory cells that have small hairs containing receptors. The gustatory receptors, like the olfactory receptors, are sensitive to specific types of dissolved chemicals. Everything we eat and drink must be dissolved—usually by saliva—in order for the gustatory receptors to identify its taste. Once dissolved, the gustatory receptors then translate a food's chemical structure before converting that information to electrical signals. These electrical signals are transmitted, via the facial and glossopharyngeal nerves, through the nose and on to the brain, where they are decoded and identified as a specific taste.

Salivation

Saliva is critical not only to the digestion of food and to the maintenance of oral hygiene but also to flavor. Saliva dissolves taste stimuli, allowing their chemistry to reach the gustatory receptor cells.

Remember being told to chew your food slowly so that you would enjoy your meal more? It's true. Tasting and chewing increase the rate of salivary flow. Taking more time to chew food and savor beverages allows more of their chemical components to dissolve and more aromas to be released. This provides more material for the gustatory and olfactory receptors to analyze, sending more complex data to the brain, which enhances perception. Taste and smell intensify.

While the majority of our taste buds are located in the mouth, we also have thousands of additional nerve endings—especially on the moist epithelial surfaces of the mouth, throat, nose, and eyes—that perceive texture, temperature, and assess a variety of factors, which recognize sensations like the prickle of sulfur, the coolness of mint, and the burn of pepper. While scientists have identified an estimated 10,000 smells, humans can detect only 2,000, and we can taste just four or five basic flavors—sweet, salty, sour, bitter, and umami (savory). Of these, only sweet, sour, and occasional bitterness are applicable to wine tasting.

The overall word for what we perceive in food and drink through a combination of smelling, tasting, and feeling is *flavor*, with smell being so predominant of the three that wine tasting is actually "wine smelling," and some chemists describe wine as "a tasteless liquid that is deeply fragrant." It is flavor that lets us know whether we are eating an apple or a pear, drinking a Puligny-Montrachet or an Australian Chardonnay. Anyone doubting the importance of smell in determining taste is encouraged to hold his or her nose while eating chocolate or cheese, either of which will tend to taste like chalk.

Taste Place

Though maps, such as the one on the next page, typically place concentrated sweet receptors at the tip of the tongue, bitter at the back, and sour at the sides, taste buds are broadly distributed throughout the mouth. In wine tasting, it is important to let wine aerate once it reaches your mouth so that it will release more aromas and intensify flavor. This is done by rolling the wine over your tongue and allowing it to linger on the tongue. This process also spreads the wine across a wider array of gustatory receptors, and gives them more time to analyze its taste. You'll discover that a good wine will reveal first, middle, and lasting impressions, which are largely determined by aroma and mouthfeel.

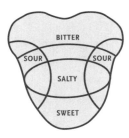

Mouthfeel

Mouthfeel is literally how a wine feels in the mouth. These feelings are characterized by sensations that delight, prick, and/or pain our tongue, lips, and cheeks, and that often linger in the mouth after swallowing or spitting. They can range from the piquant tingle of Champagne bubbles to the teeth-tightening astringency of tannin; from the cool expansiveness of menthol/eucalyptus to the heat of a high-alcohol red; and from the cloying sweetness of a low-acid white to the velvet coating of a rich Rhône. The physical feel of wine is also important to mouthfeel, and includes: body, thin to full; weight, light to heavy; and texture, austere, unctuous, silky, and chewy. Each contributes to wine's overall balance. More than just impressions, these qualities can trigger a physical response—drying, puckering, and salivation—which literally can have wines dancing on the tongue and clinging to the teeth.

You experience bitterness on the back of the tongue, on the sides, and in the throat. Bitterness in wine arises from a combination of high alcohol and high tannin. Much of what is commonly described as taste (80–90 percent or more) is aroma/bouquet as sensed and articulated by our olfactory receptors, and mouthfeel and texture as sensed by surrounding organs.

WINE TEXTURES

LIGHT: skim milk
MEDIUM: whole milk
FULL: heavy cream

A well-crafted wine's aroma evolves in the glass, and our noses quickly become inured to smell. This is why it's advisable to revisit wine's aroma a few times in any given tasting or flight. Tasters can take a cue from the old perfumer's trick of sniffing their sleeves between the many essences/elixirs they may smell on a given day. In other words, they turn to something completely different—balancing sense with non-sense.

TYPES OF TASTINGS

HORIZONTAL: Tasting wines from the same vintage

VERTICAL: Comparing wines from different vintages

BLIND: The taster does not have any information about the wines

SEMI-BLIND: The taster knows only the style of wine (grape) or where it is from

On Tasting Wine

You can read all the books (and there are plenty) on wine to become more knowledgeable on the subject, but the best way to enhance your understanding is to taste as many wines as possible. Reading covers the more academic side of wine, while tasting is more enjoyable and practical. A little of each will do you the most good. Wine tasting can be broken down into five basic steps: color, swirl, smell, taste, and savor. The following are the necessary steps for tasting wine. You may wish to follow them with a glass of wine in hand.

Color

The best way to get an idea of a wine's color is to get a white background—a napkin or tablecloth—and hold the glass of wine at an angle in front of it. The range of colors you may see depends, of course, on whether you're tasting a white or red wine. Here are the colors for both, beginning with the youngest wine and moving to an older wine:

WHITE WINE	RED WINE
Pale yellow-green	Purple
Straw yellow	
Yellow-gold	Ruby
Gold	Red
Old gold	
Yellow-brown	Brick red
Maderized	Red-brown
Brown	Brown

As white wines age, they gain color. Red wines, on the other hand, lose color as they age. If you can see through a red wine, it's generally ready to drink!

Color tells you a lot about the wine. Since we start with white wines, let's consider three reasons that a white wine may have more color:

1. It's older.
2. Different grape varieties give different color. (For example, Chardonnay usually gives off a deeper color than does Sauvignon Blanc.)
3. The wine was aged in wood.

In class, I always begin by asking my students what color the wine is. It's not unusual to hear that some believe that the wine is pale yellow-green, while others say it's gold. Everyone begins with the same wine, but color perceptions vary. There are no right or wrong answers because perception is subjective. So you can imagine what happens when we taste the wine!

Swirl

We swirl wine to allow oxygen to get into the wine. Swirling releases the esters, ethers, and aldehydes that combine with oxygen to yield a wine's bouquet. In other words, swirling aerates the wine and releases more of the bouquet and aroma. Oxygen can be the best friend of a wine, but it can also be its worst enemy. A little oxygen helps release the smell of the wine (as with swirling), but prolonged exposure can be harmful, especially to older wines.

Smell

This is the most important part of wine tasting. You can perceive just four tastes—sweet, sour, bitter, and salty—but the average person can detect more than 2,000 different scents, and wine has more than 200 of its own. Now that you've swirled the wine and released the bouquet, I want you to smell the wine at least three times. You may find that the third smell will give you more information than the first did. What does the wine smell like? What type of nose does it have? Smell is the most important step in the tasting process, and most people don't spend enough time on it.

Pinpointing the nose of the wine helps you to identify certain characteristics. The problem here is that many people want me to tell them what a wine smells like. Since I prefer not to use subjective words, I may say that the wine smells like a French white Burgundy. Still, I find that this doesn't satisfy the majority of the class. They want to know more. I ask these people to describe what steak and onions smell like. They answer, "Like steak and onions." See what I mean?

The best way to learn what your own preferences are for styles of wine is to "memorize" the smell of the individual grape varieties. For white, just try to memorize the three major grape varieties: Chardonnay, Sauvignon Blanc, and Riesling. Keep smelling them and smelling them until you can identify the differences, one from the other. For the reds it's a little more difficult, but you still can take three major grape varieties: Pinot Noir, Merlot, and Cabernet Sauvignon. Try to memorize those smells without using flowery words, and you'll understand what I'm talking about.

For those in the Wine School who remain unconvinced, I hand out a list of 500 different words commonly used to describe wine. Here is a small excerpt:

acetic	finish	oxidized
aftertaste	flat	pétillant
aroma	fresh	rich
astringent	grapey	seductive
austere	green	short
baked-burnt	hard	stalky
balanced	hot	sulfury
bitter	legs	tart
body	light	thin
bouquet	maderized	tired
bright	mature	vanilla
character	metallic	woody
corky	nose	yeasty
developed	nutty	young
earthy	off	

Other sensations associated with wine include numbing, tingling, drying, cooling, warming, and coating. *WineSpeak* by Bernard Klem includes 36,975 wine-tasting descriptions. Who knew?

I like to have my students put their hands over the glass of wine when they swirl to create a more powerful bouquet and aroma. Bouquet is the total smell of the wine. Aroma is the smell of the grapes. *Nose* is a word that wine tasters use to describe the bouquet and aroma of the wine.

You're more likely to recognize some of the defects of a wine through your sense of smell. Following is a list of some of the negative smells in wine:

SMELL	WHY
Vinegar	Too much acetic acid in wine
Sherry*	Oxidation
Dank, wet, moldy, cellar smell	Defective cork
Sulfur (burnt matches)	Too much sulfur dioxide

* Authentic Sherry, from Spain, is intentionally made through controlled oxidation.

All wines contain some sulfur dioxide, since it is a natural byproduct of fermentation. Sulfur dioxide also is used in winemaking. It kills bacteria, prevents unwanted fermentation, and acts as a preservative. It sometimes causes a burning and itching sensation in your nose.

Each person has a different threshold for sulfur dioxide, and although most people do not have an adverse reaction, it can be a problem for individuals with asthma. To protect those who are prone to bad reactions to sulfites, federal law in the United States requires wineries to label their wines with the warning that the wine contains sulfites.

Taste

To many people, tasting wine means taking a sip and swallowing immediately. To me, this isn't tasting. Tasting is something you do with your taste buds. Tasting wine is confirming what the color and smell are telling you. You have taste buds all over your mouth—on both sides of the tongue, underneath, on the tip, and extending to the back of your throat. If you do what many people do, you take a gulp of wine and bypass all of those important taste buds. When I taste wine I leave it in my mouth for three to five seconds before swallowing. The wine warms up, sending signals about the bouquet and aroma up through the nasal passage then on to the olfactory bulb, and then to the limbic system of the brain. Remember, 90 percent of taste is smell.

What should you think about when tasting wine?

Be aware of the most important sensations of taste and your own personal thresholds of those tastes. Also, pay attention to where they occur on your tongue and in your mouth. As I mentioned earlier, you can perceive just four tastes: sweet, sour, bitter, and salty (but there's no salt in wine, so we're down to three). Bitterness in wine is usually created by high alcohol and high tannin. Sweetness occurs only in wines that have some residual sugar left over after fermentation. Sour (sometimes called "tart") indicates the acidity in wine.

SWEETNESS: The highest threshold is on the tip of the tongue. If there's any sweetness in a wine whatsoever, you'll get it right away.

ACIDITY: Found at the sides of the tongue, the cheek area, and the back of the throat. White wines and some lighter-style red wines usually contain a higher degree of acidity.

BITTERNESS: Tasted on the back of the tongue.

TANNIN: The sensation of tannin begins in the middle of the tongue. Tannin frequently exists in red wines or white wines aged in wood. When the wines are too young, tannin dries the palate to excess. If there's a lot of tannin in the wine, it can actually coat your whole mouth, blocking the fruit. Remember, tannin is not a taste: it is a tactile sensation.

FRUIT AND VARIETAL CHARACTERISTICS: These are not tastes, but smells. The weight of the fruit (the "body") will be felt in the middle of the tongue.

AFTERTASTE: The overall taste and balance of the components of the wine that lingers in your mouth. How long does the balance last? Usually a sign of a high-quality wine is a long, pleasing aftertaste. The taste of many of the great wines lasts anywhere from one to three minutes, with all their components in harmony.

Savor

After you've had a chance to taste the wine, sit back for a few moments and savor it. Think about what you just experienced and ask yourself the following questions to help focus your impressions:

- Was the wine light, medium, or full-bodied?
- For a white wine: How was the acidity? Very little, just right, or too much?
- For a red wine: Is the tannin in the wine too strong or astringent?

- What is the strongest component (residual sugar, fruit, acid, tannin)?

- How long did the balance of the components last (ten seconds, sixty seconds, etc.)?

- Is the wine ready to drink? Or does it need more time to age?

- What kind of food would you enjoy with the wine?

- To your taste, is the wine worth the price?

- This brings us to the most important point. The first thing you should consider after you've tasted a wine is whether or not you like it. Is it your style?

You can compare tasting wine to browsing in an art gallery. You wander from room to room looking at the paintings. Your first impression tells whether you like something. Once you decide you like a work of art, you want to know more: Who was the artist? What is the history behind the piece? How was it made? So it is with wine. Usually, once oenophiles (wine aficionados) discover a wine that they like, they want to learn everything about it: the winemaker; the grapes; exactly where the vines were planted; the blend, if any; and the history behind the wine.

THE 60-SECOND WINE EXPERT

Over the last few years I have insisted that my students spend one minute in silence after they swallow the wine. I use a "60-second wine expert" tasting sheet in my classes for students to record their impressions. The minute is divided into four sections: 0 to 15 seconds, 15 to 30 seconds, 30 to 45 seconds, and the final 45 to 60 seconds. Try this with your next glass of wine.

The first taste of wine is a shock to your taste buds. This is due to the alcohol content, acidity, and sometimes the tannin in the wine. The higher the alcohol or acidity, the more of a shock. For the first wine in any tasting, it is probably best to take a sip and swirl it around in your mouth, but don't evaluate it. Wait another 30 seconds, try it again, and then begin the 60-second wine expert tasting.

0 TO 15 SECONDS: If there is any residual sugar/sweetness in the wine, you will experience it now. If there is no sweetness in the wine, the acidity is usually its strongest sensation in the first 15 seconds.

Look for the fruit level of the wine and its balance with the acidity or sweetness.

15 TO 30 SECONDS: After the sweetness or acidity, look for great fruit sensation. After all, that is what you're paying for! By the time you reach 30 seconds, you are hoping for balance of all the components. By this time, you can identify the weight of the wine. Is it light, medium, or full-bodied? Starting thinking about what kind of food to pair with this wine.

30 TO 45 SECONDS: Start formulating your opinion of the wine and whether you like it. Not all wines need 60 seconds of thought. Lighter-style wines, such as Rieslings, will usually show their best at this point. The fruit, acid, and sweetness of a great German Riesling should be in perfect harmony from this point on. For quality red and white wines, acidity—which is a very strong component, especially in the first 30 seconds—should now be in balance with the fruit of the wine.

45 TO 60 SECONDS: Very often wine writers use the term *length* to describe how long the components, balance, and flavor continue in the mouth. Concentrate on the length of the wine in these last 15 seconds. In big, full-bodied red wines from Bordeaux and the Rhône Valley, Cabernets from California, Barolos and Barbarescos from Italy, and even some full-bodied Chardonnays, concentrate on the level of tannin in the wine.

Just as the acidity and fruit balance are your major concerns in the first 30 seconds, it is now the tannin and fruit balance you are looking for in the last 30 seconds. If the fruit, tannin, and acid are all in balance at 60 seconds, then the wine is probably ready to drink. Does the tannin overpower the fruit? If it does at the 60-second mark, consider whether to drink the wine now or put it away for more aging.

It is extremely important, if you want to learn the true taste of the wine, that you take at least one minute to concentrate on all of its components. In my classes it is amazing to see more than a hundred students silently taking one minute to analyze a wine. Some close their eyes, some bow their heads in deep thought, others write notes.

One final point: 60 seconds is the *minimum* time to wait before making a decision about a wine. Many great wines continue to show balance well past 120 seconds. The best wine I ever tasted lasted more than three minutes—that's three minutes of perfect balance of all components!

STEP ONE: Look at the color of the wine.

STEP TWO: Smell the wine three times.

STEP THREE: Put the wine in your mouth and leave it there for three to five seconds.

STEP FOUR: Swallow the wine.

STEP FIVE: Wait and concentrate on the wine for 60 seconds before discussing it.

GLOSSARY OF SELECT TERMS

ACID: One of the components of wine. It is sometimes described as sour or tart and can be found on the sides of the tongue and mouth.

AFTERTASTE: The sensation in the mouth that persists after the wine has been swallowed.

AOC: Abbreviation for *Appellation d'Origine Contrôlée;* the French government laws that control wine production.

AROMA: The smell of the grapes in a wine.

ASTRINGENT: The mouthfeel created by tannins in wine.

AVA: American Viticultural Area, a designated wine-producing area in the United States.

BARREL-FERMENTED: Describes wine that has been fermented in small oak barrels rather than in stainless steel. The oak from a barrel will add complexity to a wine's flavor and texture.

BLEND: A combination of two or more wines or grapes, to enhance flavor, balance, and complexity.

BRUT: A French term used for the driest style of Champagne and/or sparkling wine.

COLHEITA ("coal-AY-ta"): "vintage" in Portuguese.

CRU: Certain vineyards in France are designated Grand Cru and Premier Cru, the classification indicating level of quality.

Cuvée: From the French *cuve* (vat); may refer to a particular blend of grapes or, in Champagne, to the select portion of the juice from the pressing of the grapes.

DEMI-SEC ("deh-mee-SECK"): A Champagne containing a higher level of residual sugar than a brut.

DOC: Abbreviation for *Denominazione di Origine Controllata*, the Italian laws that control wine production. Spain also uses this abbreviation for *Denominación de Origen Condado*.

DOCG: Abbreviation for *Denominazione di Origine Controllata e Garantita*; the Italian government allows this marking to appear only on the finest Italian wines. The *G* stands for *guaranteed*.

DRY: Wine containing very little residual sugar. It is the opposite of sweet, in wine terms.

ESTATE-BOTTLED: Wine made, produced, and bottled on the estate where the grapes were grown.

EXTRA DRY: Less dry than brut Champagne.

FINO ("FEE-noh"): A type of Sherry.

FINISH: The taste and feel that wine leaves in the mouth after swallowing. Some wines disappear immediately while others can linger for some time.

GRAND CRU ("grawn crew"): The highest classification for wines in Burgundy.

GRAND CRU CLASSÉ ("grawn crew clas-SAY"): The highest level of the Bordeaux classification.

GRAN RESERVA: A Spanish wine that has had extra aging.

HALBTROCKEN: The German term meaning "semidry."

KABINETT ("kah-bee-NETT"): A light, semidry German wine.

MALOLACTIC FERMENTATION: A secondary fermentation process wherein malic acid is converted into lactic acid and carbon dioxide. This process reduces the wine's acidity and adds complexity.

MERITAGE: Trademark designation for specific high-quality American wines containing the same blend of varieties that are used in the making of Bordeaux wines in France.

MÉTHODE CHAMPENOISE ("may-TUD shahm-pen-WAHZ"): The method by which Champagne, and sometimes sparkling wine, is made.

PRÄDIKATSWEIN ("pray-dee-KAHTS-vine"): The highest level of quality in German wines.

PREMIER CRU: A wine that has special characteristics and that comes from a specific designated vineyard in Burgundy, France, or is blended from several such vineyards.

QUALITÄTSWEIN ("kval-ee-TATES-vine"): A German term meaning "quality wine."

TERROIR: All the elements that contribute to the distinctive characteristics of a particular vineyard site, including its soil, subsoil, slope, drainage, elevation, and climate, as well as the exposure to the sun, temperature, and precipitation.

VARIETAL WINE: A wine that is labeled with the predominant grape used to produce the wine. For example, a wine made from Chardonnay grapes would be labeled "Chardonnay."

VINTAGE: The year the grapes are harvested.

FURTHER READING

For more information on the topics discussed in this notebook, see:

KEVIN ZRALY WINDOWS ON THE WORLD
COMPLETE WINE COURSE:
30TH ANNIVERSARY EDITION
Cooking/Beverages/Wine & Spirits
ISBN 978-1-4549-1364-1

For more information about Kevin Zraly and the Windows on the World Wine School, visit KevinZraly.com

TASTING SHEETS

TASTING NOTES   DATE   /   /

NAME ....

VINTAGE .... COUNTRY/REGION ....

PRICE .... GRAPES ....

COLOR .... (P. 59)

AROMAS / BOUQUET .... (P. 6–7)

FLAVORS .... (P. 62)

COLOR (P. 59)
AROMAS / BOUQUET (P. 6–7)
FLAVORS (P. 62)

CHECKLIST

	BODY/TEXTURE	FRUIT		RESIDUAL SUGAR	ACID	TANNIN
LIGHT	○	○	LOW	○	○	○
MEDIUM	○	○	BALANCED	○	○	○
FULL	○	○	HIGH	○	○	○

60-SECOND WINE TASTING

0–15 SECONDS ....

15–30 SECONDS ....

30–45 SECONDS ....

45–60 SECONDS ....

NOTES/FOOD CHOICES

....

....

OVERALL RATING

POOR   ACCEPTABLE   GOOD   EXCELLENT   EXCEPTIONAL
 ○   ○   ○   ○   ○

TASTING NOTES   DATE   /   /

NAME

VINTAGE   COUNTRY/REGION

PRICE   GRAPES

COLOR   (P. 59)

AROMAS / BOUQUET   (P. 6-7)

FLAVORS   (P. 62)

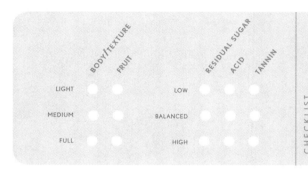

	BODY/TEXTURE	FRUIT		RESIDUAL SUGAR	ACID	TANNIN
LIGHT	○	○	LOW	○	○	○
MEDIUM	○	○	BALANCED	○	○	○
FULL	○	○	HIGH	○	○	○

CHECKLIST

60-SECOND WINE TASTING

0-15 SECONDS

15-30 SECONDS

30-45 SECONDS

45-60 SECONDS

NOTES/FOOD CHOICES

OVERALL RATING

POOR   ACCEPTABLE   GOOD   EXCELLENT   EXCEPTIONAL

NAME

VINTAGE   COUNTRY/REGION

PRICE   GRAPES

COLOR   (P. 59)

AROMAS / BOUQUET   (P. 6–7)

FLAVORS   (P. 62)

CHECKLIST

	BODY/TEXTURE	FRUIT		RESIDUAL SUGAR	ACID	TANNIN
LIGHT	○	○	LOW	○	○	○
MEDIUM	○	○	BALANCED	○	○	○
FULL	○	○	HIGH	○	○	○

60-SECOND WINE TASTING

0–15 SECONDS

15–30 SECONDS

30–45 SECONDS

45–60 SECONDS

NOTES/FOOD CHOICES

OVERALL RATING

POOR   ACCEPTABLE   GOOD   EXCELLENT   EXCEPTIONAL

TASTING NOTES

DATE   /   /

NAME

VINTAGE   COUNTRY/REGION

PRICE   GRAPES

COLOR   (P. 59)

AROMAS / BOUQUET   (P. 6–7)

FLAVORS   (P. 62)

	BODY/TEXTURE	FRUIT		RESIDUAL SUGAR	ACID	TANNIN
LIGHT	○	○	LOW	○	○	○
MEDIUM	○	○	BALANCED	○	○	○
FULL	○	○	HIGH	○	○	○

CHECKLIST

60-SECOND WINE TASTING

0–15 SECONDS

15–30 SECONDS

30–45 SECONDS

45–60 SECONDS

NOTES/FOOD CHOICES

OVERALL RATING

POOR   ACCEPTABLE   GOOD   EXCELLENT   EXCEPTIONAL

🍇 TASTING NOTES

DATE   /   /

NAME

VINTAGE   COUNTRY/REGION

PRICE   GRAPES

COLOR   (P. 59)

AROMAS / BOUQUET   (P. 6–7)

FLAVORS   (P. 62)

CHECKLIST

	BODY/TEXTURE	FRUIT		RESIDUAL SUGAR	ACID	TANNIN
LIGHT	○	○	LOW	○	○	○
MEDIUM	○	○	BALANCED	○	○	○
FULL	○	○	HIGH	○	○	○

60-SECOND WINE TASTING

0–15 SECONDS

15–30 SECONDS

30–45 SECONDS

45–60 SECONDS

NOTES/FOOD CHOICES

OVERALL RATING

POOR   ACCEPTABLE   GOOD   EXCELLENT   EXCEPTIONAL

TASTING NOTES

DATE   /   /

NAME

VINTAGE   COUNTRY/REGION

PRICE   GRAPES

COLOR   (P. 59)

AROMAS / BOUQUET   (P. 6–7)

FLAVORS   (P. 62)

	BODY/TEXTURE	FRUIT		RESIDUAL SUGAR	ACID	TANNIN	
LIGHT	○	○	LOW	○	○	○	CHECKLIST
MEDIUM	○	○	BALANCED	○	○	○	
FULL	○	○	HIGH	○	○	○	

60-SECOND WINE TASTING

0–15 SECONDS

15–30 SECONDS

30–45 SECONDS

45–60 SECONDS

NOTES/FOOD CHOICES

OVERALL RATING

POOR   ACCEPTABLE   GOOD   EXCELLENT   EXCEPTIONAL

TASTING NOTES   DATE   /   /

NAME

VINTAGE   COUNTRY/REGION

PRICE   GRAPES

COLOR   (P. 59)

AROMAS / BOUQUET   (P. 6-7)

FLAVORS   (P. 62)

CHECKLIST

	BODY/TEXTURE	FRUIT		RESIDUAL SUGAR	ACID	TANNIN
LIGHT	○	○	LOW	○	○	○
MEDIUM	○	○	BALANCED	○	○	○
FULL	○	○	HIGH	○	○	○

60-SECOND WINE TASTING

0-15 SECONDS

15-30 SECONDS

30-45 SECONDS

45-60 SECONDS

NOTES/FOOD CHOICES

OVERALL RATING

POOR   ACCEPTABLE   GOOD   EXCELLENT   EXCEPTIONAL

TASTING NOTES   DATE   /   /

NAME

VINTAGE   COUNTRY/REGION

PRICE   GRAPES

COLOR   (P. 59)

AROMAS / BOUQUET   (P. 6-7)

FLAVORS   (P. 62)

	BODY/TEXTURE	FRUIT			RESIDUAL SUGAR	ACID	TANNIN
LIGHT	○	○		LOW	○	○	○
MEDIUM	○	○		BALANCED	○	○	○
FULL	○	○		HIGH	○	○	○

CHECKLIST

60-SECOND WINE TASTING

0-15 SECONDS

15-30 SECONDS

30-45 SECONDS

45-60 SECONDS

NOTES/FOOD CHOICES

OVERALL RATING

POOR   ACCEPTABLE   GOOD   EXCELLENT   EXCEPTIONAL

TASTING NOTES DATE / /

NAME

VINTAGE   COUNTRY/REGION

PRICE   GRAPES

COLOR   (P. 59)

AROMAS / BOUQUET   (P. 6–7)

FLAVORS   (P. 62)

CHECKLIST

	BODY/TEXTURE	FRUIT		RESIDUAL SUGAR	ACID	TANNIN
LIGHT	○	○	LOW	○	○	○
MEDIUM	○	○	BALANCED	○	○	○
FULL	○	○	HIGH	○	○	○

60-SECOND WINE TASTING

0–15 SECONDS

15–30 SECONDS

30–45 SECONDS

45–60 SECONDS

NOTES/FOOD CHOICES

OVERALL RATING

POOR   ACCEPTABLE   GOOD   EXCELLENT   EXCEPTIONAL

TASTING NOTES

DATE   /   /

NAME

VINTAGE   COUNTRY/REGION

PRICE   GRAPES

COLOR   (P. 59)

AROMAS / BOUQUET   (P. 6–7)

FLAVORS   (P. 62)

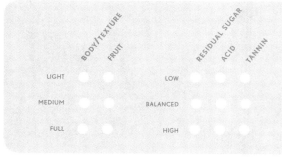

60-SECOND WINE TASTING

0–15 SECONDS

15–30 SECONDS

30–45 SECONDS

45–60 SECONDS

NOTES/FOOD CHOICES

OVERALL RATING

POOR   ACCEPTABLE   GOOD   EXCELLENT   EXCEPTIONAL

TASTING NOTES

DATE / /

NAME

VINTAGE   COUNTRY/REGION

PRICE   GRAPES

COLOR   (P. 59)

AROMAS / BOUQUET   (P. 6-7)

FLAVORS   (P. 62)

CHECKLIST

	BODY/TEXTURE	FRUIT		RESIDUAL SUGAR	ACID	TANNIN
LIGHT	○	○	LOW	○	○	○
MEDIUM	○	○	BALANCED	○	○	○
FULL	○	○	HIGH	○	○	○

60-SECOND WINE TASTING

0-15 SECONDS

15-30 SECONDS

30-45 SECONDS

45-60 SECONDS

NOTES/FOOD CHOICES

OVERALL RATING

POOR   ACCEPTABLE   GOOD   EXCELLENT   EXCEPTIONAL

TASTING NOTES

DATE   /   /

NAME ....

VINTAGE .... COUNTRY/REGION ....

PRICE .... GRAPES ....

COLOR .... (P. 59)

AROMAS / BOUQUET .... (P. 6–7)

FLAVORS .... (P. 62)

(P. 59)

(P. 6–7)

(P. 62)

	BODY/TEXTURE	FRUIT		RESIDUAL SUGAR	ACID	TANNIN
LIGHT	○	○	LOW	○	○	○
MEDIUM	○	○	BALANCED	○	○	○
FULL	○	○	HIGH	○	○	○

CHECKLIST

60-SECOND WINE TASTING

0–15 SECONDS ....

15–30 SECONDS ....

30–45 SECONDS ....

45–60 SECONDS ....

NOTES/FOOD CHOICES

....

....

OVERALL RATING

POOR   ACCEPTABLE   GOOD   EXCELLENT   EXCEPTIONAL

TASTING NOTES

DATE   /   /

NAME

VINTAGE   COUNTRY/REGION

PRICE   GRAPES

COLOR   (P. 59)

AROMAS / BOUQUET   (P. 6–7)

FLAVORS   (P. 62)

CHECKLIST

	BODY/TEXTURE	FRUIT			RESIDUAL SUGAR	ACID	TANNIN
LIGHT	○	○	LOW		○	○	○
MEDIUM	○	○	BALANCED		○	○	○
FULL	○	○	HIGH		○	○	○

60-SECOND WINE TASTING

0–15 SECONDS

15–30 SECONDS

30–45 SECONDS

45–60 SECONDS

NOTES/FOOD CHOICES

OVERALL RATING

POOR   ACCEPTABLE   GOOD   EXCELLENT   EXCEPTIONAL

TASTING NOTES   DATE   /   /

NAME ....

VINTAGE .... COUNTRY/REGION ....

PRICE .... GRAPES ....

COLOR .... (P. 59)

AROMAS / BOUQUET .... (P. 6–7)

FLAVORS .... (P. 62)

	BODY/TEXTURE	FRUIT			RESIDUAL SUGAR	ACID	TANNIN
LIGHT	○	○	LOW		○	○	○
MEDIUM	○	○	BALANCED		○	○	○
FULL	○	○	HIGH		○	○	○

CHECKLIST

60-SECOND WINE TASTING

0–15 SECONDS ....

15–30 SECONDS ....

30–45 SECONDS ....

45–60 SECONDS ....

NOTES/FOOD CHOICES
....
....

OVERALL RATING

POOR   ACCEPTABLE   GOOD   EXCELLENT   EXCEPTIONAL
 ○   ○   ○   ○   ○

TASTING NOTES   DATE   /   /

NAME ....

VINTAGE .... COUNTRY/REGION ....

PRICE .... GRAPES ....

COLOR .... (P. 59)

AROMAS / BOUQUET .... (P. 6-7)

FLAVORS .... (P. 62)

CHECKLIST

	BODY/TEXTURE	FRUIT		RESIDUAL SUGAR	ACID	TANNIN
LIGHT	○	○	LOW	○	○	○
MEDIUM	○	○	BALANCED	○	○	○
FULL	○	○	HIGH	○	○	○

60-SECOND WINE TASTING

0-15 SECONDS ....

15-30 SECONDS ....

30-45 SECONDS ....

45-60 SECONDS ....

NOTES/FOOD CHOICES

....

....

OVERALL RATING

POOR   ACCEPTABLE   GOOD   EXCELLENT   EXCEPTIONAL
○   ○   ○   ○   ○

TASTING NOTES   DATE   /   /

NAME ....

VINTAGE .... COUNTRY/REGION ....

PRICE .... GRAPES ....

COLOR .... (P. 59)

AROMAS / BOUQUET .... (P. 6–7)

FLAVORS .... (P. 62)

	BODY/TEXTURE	FRUIT			RESIDUAL SUGAR	ACID	TANNIN
LIGHT	○	○		LOW	○	○	○
MEDIUM	○	○		BALANCED	○	○	○
FULL	○	○		HIGH	○	○	○

CHECKLIST

60-SECOND WINE TASTING

0–15 SECONDS ....

15–30 SECONDS ....

30–45 SECONDS ....

45–60 SECONDS ....

NOTES/FOOD CHOICES

....

....

OVERALL RATING

POOR   ACCEPTABLE   GOOD   EXCELLENT   EXCEPTIONAL
○   ○   ○   ○   ○

TASTING NOTES

DATE   /   /

NAME _____

VINTAGE _____ COUNTRY/REGION _____

PRICE _____ GRAPES _____

COLOR _____ (P. 59)

AROMAS / BOUQUET _____ (P. 6–7)

FLAVORS _____ (P. 62)

CHECKLIST

	BODY/TEXTURE	FRUIT		RESIDUAL SUGAR	ACID	TANNIN
LIGHT	○	○	LOW	○	○	○
MEDIUM	○	○	BALANCED	○	○	○
FULL	○	○	HIGH	○	○	○

60-SECOND WINE TASTING

0–15 SECONDS _____

15–30 SECONDS _____

30–45 SECONDS _____

45–60 SECONDS _____

NOTES/FOOD CHOICES

....

....

OVERALL RATING

POOR   ACCEPTABLE   GOOD   EXCELLENT   EXCEPTIONAL
  ○   ○   ○   ○   ○

TASTING NOTES   DATE   /   /

NAME

VINTAGE   COUNTRY/REGION

PRICE   GRAPES

COLOR   (P. 59)

AROMAS / BOUQUET   (P. 6-7)

FLAVORS   (P. 62)

	BODY/TEXTURE	FRUIT		RESIDUAL SUGAR	ACID	TANNIN
LIGHT	○	○	LOW	○	○	○
MEDIUM	○	○	BALANCED	○	○	○
FULL	○	○	HIGH	○	○	○

CHECKLIST

60-SECOND WINE TASTING

0-15 SECONDS

15-30 SECONDS

30-45 SECONDS

45-60 SECONDS

NOTES/FOOD CHOICES

OVERALL RATING

POOR   ACCEPTABLE   GOOD   EXCELLENT   EXCEPTIONAL

TASTING NOTES

DATE / /

NAME

VINTAGE   COUNTRY/REGION

PRICE   GRAPES

COLOR   (P. 59)

AROMAS / BOUQUET   (P. 6-7)

FLAVORS   (P. 62)

CHECKLIST

	BODY/TEXTURE	FRUIT		RESIDUAL SUGAR	ACID	TANNIN
LIGHT	○	○	LOW	○	○	○
MEDIUM	○	○	BALANCED	○	○	○
FULL	○	○	HIGH	○	○	○

60-SECOND WINE TASTING

0-15 SECONDS

15-30 SECONDS

30-45 SECONDS

45-60 SECONDS

NOTES/FOOD CHOICES

OVERALL RATING

POOR   ACCEPTABLE   GOOD   EXCELLENT   EXCEPTIONAL

TASTING NOTES   DATE   /   /

NAME

VINTAGE   COUNTRY/REGION

PRICE   GRAPES

COLOR   (P. 59)

AROMAS / BOUQUET   (P. 6-7)

FLAVORS   (P. 62)

	BODY/TEXTURE	FRUIT		RESIDUAL SUGAR	ACID	TANNIN
LIGHT	○	○	LOW	○	○	○
MEDIUM	○	○	BALANCED	○	○	○
FULL	○	○	HIGH	○	○	○

CHECKLIST

60-SECOND WINE TASTING

0-15 SECONDS

15-30 SECONDS

30-45 SECONDS

45-60 SECONDS

NOTES/FOOD CHOICES

OVERALL RATING

POOR   ACCEPTABLE   GOOD   EXCELLENT   EXCEPTIONAL
  ○   ○   ○   ○   ○

🍇 TASTING NOTES DATE / /

NAME ....

VINTAGE .... COUNTRY/REGION ....

PRICE .... GRAPES ....

COLOR .... (P. 59)

AROMAS / BOUQUET .... (P. 6-7)

FLAVORS .... (P. 62)

CHECKLIST

	BODY/TEXTURE	FRUIT		RESIDUAL SUGAR	ACID	TANNIN
LIGHT	○	○	LOW	○	○	○
MEDIUM	○	○	BALANCED	○	○	○
FULL	○	○	HIGH	○	○	○

60-SECOND WINE TASTING

0-15 SECONDS ....

15-30 SECONDS ....

30-45 SECONDS ....

45-60 SECONDS ....

NOTES/FOOD CHOICES

....

....

OVERALL RATING

POOR   ACCEPTABLE   GOOD   EXCELLENT   EXCEPTIONAL
 ○   ○   ○   ○   ○

TASTING NOTES   DATE   /   /

NAME ....

VINTAGE .... COUNTRY/REGION ....

PRICE .... GRAPES ....

COLOR .... (P. 59)

AROMAS / BOUQUET .... (P. 6–7)

FLAVORS .... (P. 62)

	BODY/TEXTURE	FRUIT		RESIDUAL SUGAR	ACID	TANNIN
LIGHT	◯	◯	LOW	◯	◯	◯
MEDIUM	◯	◯	BALANCED	◯	◯	◯
FULL	◯	◯	HIGH	◯	◯	◯

CHECKLIST

60-SECOND WINE TASTING

0–15 SECONDS ....

15–30 SECONDS ....

30–45 SECONDS ....

45–60 SECONDS ....

NOTES/FOOD CHOICES

....

....

OVERALL RATING

POOR   ACCEPTABLE   GOOD   EXCELLENT   EXCEPTIONAL

TASTING NOTES

DATE   /   /

NAME

VINTAGE   COUNTRY/REGION

PRICE   GRAPES

COLOR   (P. 59)

AROMAS / BOUQUET   (P. 6-7)

FLAVORS   (P. 62)

CHECKLIST

	BODY/TEXTURE	FRUIT		RESIDUAL SUGAR	ACID	TANNIN
LIGHT	○	○	LOW	○	○	○
MEDIUM	○	○	BALANCED	○	○	○
FULL	○	○	HIGH	○	○	○

60-SECOND WINE TASTING

0-15 SECONDS

15-30 SECONDS

30-45 SECONDS

45-60 SECONDS

NOTES/FOOD CHOICES

OVERALL RATING

POOR   ACCEPTABLE   GOOD   EXCELLENT   EXCEPTIONAL

TASTING NOTES

DATE   /   /

NAME

VINTAGE   COUNTRY/REGION

PRICE   GRAPES

COLOR   (P. 59)

AROMAS / BOUQUET   (P. 6-7)

FLAVORS   (P. 62)

	BODY/TEXTURE	FRUIT			RESIDUAL SUGAR	ACID	TANNIN
LIGHT	○	○	LOW		○	○	○
MEDIUM	○	○	BALANCED		○	○	○
FULL	○	○	HIGH		○	○	○

CHECKLIST

60-SECOND WINE TASTING

0-15 SECONDS

15-30 SECONDS

30-45 SECONDS

45-60 SECONDS

NOTES/FOOD CHOICES

OVERALL RATING

POOR   ACCEPTABLE   GOOD   EXCELLENT   EXCEPTIONAL
○   ○   ○   ○   ○

TASTING NOTES

DATE   /   /

NAME

VINTAGE   COUNTRY/REGION

PRICE   GRAPES

COLOR   (P. 59)

AROMAS / BOUQUET   (P. 6-7)

FLAVORS   (P. 62)

CHECKLIST

	BODY/TEXTURE	FRUIT		RESIDUAL SUGAR	ACID	TANNIN
LIGHT	○	○	LOW	○	○	○
MEDIUM	○	○	BALANCED	○	○	○
FULL	○	○	HIGH	○	○	○

60-SECOND WINE TASTING

0-15 SECONDS

15-30 SECONDS

30-45 SECONDS

45-60 SECONDS

NOTES/FOOD CHOICES

OVERALL RATING

POOR   ACCEPTABLE   GOOD   EXCELLENT   EXCEPTIONAL

NAME

VINTAGE   COUNTRY/REGION

PRICE   GRAPES

COLOR   (P. 59)

AROMAS / BOUQUET   (P. 6–7)

FLAVORS   (P. 62)

	BODY/TEXTURE	FRUIT		RESIDUAL SUGAR	ACID	TANNIN
LIGHT	○	○	LOW	○	○	○
MEDIUM	○	○	BALANCED	○	○	○
FULL	○	○	HIGH	○	○	○

CHECKLIST

60-SECOND WINE TASTING

0–15 SECONDS

15–30 SECONDS

30–45 SECONDS

45–60 SECONDS

NOTES/FOOD CHOICES

OVERALL RATING

POOR	ACCEPTABLE	GOOD	EXCELLENT	EXCEPTIONAL
○	○	○	○	○

TASTING NOTES

DATE   /   /

NAME

VINTAGE   COUNTRY/REGION

PRICE   GRAPES

COLOR   (P. 59)

AROMAS / BOUQUET   (P. 6-7)

FLAVORS   (P. 62)

CHECKLIST

	BODY/TEXTURE	FRUIT		RESIDUAL SUGAR	ACID	TANNIN
LIGHT	○	○	LOW	○	○	○
MEDIUM	○	○	BALANCED	○	○	○
FULL	○	○	HIGH	○	○	○

60-SECOND WINE TASTING

0-15 SECONDS

15-30 SECONDS

30-45 SECONDS

45-60 SECONDS

NOTES/FOOD CHOICES

OVERALL RATING

POOR   ACCEPTABLE   GOOD   EXCELLENT   EXCEPTIONAL

TASTING NOTES DATE / /

NAME

VINTAGE COUNTRY/REGION

PRICE GRAPES

COLOR (P. 59)

AROMAS / BOUQUET (P. 6-7)

FLAVORS (P. 62)

	BODY/TEXTURE	FRUIT		RESIDUAL SUGAR	ACID	TANNIN
LIGHT	○	○	LOW	○	○	○
MEDIUM	○	○	BALANCED	○	○	○
FULL	○	○	HIGH	○	○	○

CHECKLIST

60-SECOND WINE TASTING

0-15 SECONDS

15-30 SECONDS

30-45 SECONDS

45-60 SECONDS

NOTES/FOOD CHOICES

OVERALL RATING

POOR ACCEPTABLE GOOD EXCELLENT EXCEPTIONAL

🍇 TASTING NOTES   DATE   /   /

NAME

VINTAGE   COUNTRY/REGION

PRICE   GRAPES

COLOR   (P. 59)

AROMAS / BOUQUET   (P. 6-7)

FLAVORS   (P. 62)

CHECKLIST

	BODY/TEXTURE	FRUIT		RESIDUAL SUGAR	ACID	TANNIN
LIGHT	○	○	LOW	○	○	○
MEDIUM	○	○	BALANCED	○	○	○
FULL	○	○	HIGH	○	○	○

60-SECOND WINE TASTING

0-15 SECONDS

15-30 SECONDS

30-45 SECONDS

45-60 SECONDS

NOTES/FOOD CHOICES

OVERALL RATING

POOR   ACCEPTABLE   GOOD   EXCELLENT   EXCEPTIONAL
 ●   ●   ●   ●   ●

TASTING NOTES   DATE   /   /

NAME

VINTAGE   COUNTRY/REGION

PRICE   GRAPES

COLOR   (P. 59)

AROMAS / BOUQUET   (P. 6–7)

FLAVORS   (P. 62)

	BODY/TEXTURE	FRUIT		RESIDUAL SUGAR	ACID	TANNIN
LIGHT	●	●	LOW	●	●	●
MEDIUM	●	●	BALANCED	●	●	●
FULL	●	●	HIGH	●	●	●

CHECKLIST

60-SECOND WINE TASTING

0–15 SECONDS

15–30 SECONDS

30–45 SECONDS

45–60 SECONDS

NOTES/FOOD CHOICES

OVERALL RATING

POOR   ACCEPTABLE   GOOD   EXCELLENT   EXCEPTIONAL
●   ●   ●   ●   ●

TASTING NOTES

DATE   /   /

NAME

VINTAGE   COUNTRY/REGION

PRICE   GRAPES

COLOR   (P. 59)

AROMAS / BOUQUET   (P. 6–7)

FLAVORS   (P. 62)

CHECKLIST

	BODY/TEXTURE	FRUIT		RESIDUAL SUGAR	ACID	TANNIN
LIGHT	◯	◯	LOW	◯	◯	◯
MEDIUM	◯	◯	BALANCED	◯	◯	◯
FULL	◯	◯	HIGH	◯	◯	◯

60-SECOND WINE TASTING

0–15 SECONDS

15–30 SECONDS

30–45 SECONDS

45–60 SECONDS

NOTES/FOOD CHOICES

OVERALL RATING

POOR   ACCEPTABLE   GOOD   EXCELLENT   EXCEPTIONAL

TASTING NOTES   DATE   /   /

NAME
....

VINTAGE   COUNTRY/REGION
....

PRICE   GRAPES
....

COLOR   (P. 59)
....

AROMAS / BOUQUET   (P. 6–7)
....

FLAVORS   (P. 62)
....

	BODY/TEXTURE	FRUIT			RESIDUAL SUGAR	ACID	TANNIN
LIGHT	○	○		LOW	○	○	○
MEDIUM	○	○		BALANCED	○	○	○
FULL	○	○		HIGH	○	○	○

CHECKLIST

60-SECOND WINE TASTING

0–15 SECONDS
....

15–30 SECONDS
....

30–45 SECONDS
....

45–60 SECONDS

NOTES/FOOD CHOICES
....
....

OVERALL RATING

POOR   ACCEPTABLE   GOOD   EXCELLENT   EXCEPTIONAL
 ○   ○   ○   ○   ○

🍇 TASTING NOTES

DATE   /   /

NAME

VINTAGE   COUNTRY/REGION

PRICE   GRAPES

COLOR   (P. 59)

AROMAS / BOUQUET   (P. 6–7)

FLAVORS   (P. 62)

CHECKLIST

	BODY/TEXTURE	FRUIT		RESIDUAL SUGAR	ACID	TANNIN
LIGHT	○	○	LOW	○	○	○
MEDIUM	○	○	BALANCED	○	○	○
FULL	○	○	HIGH	○	○	○

60-SECOND WINE TASTING

0–15 SECONDS

15–30 SECONDS

30–45 SECONDS

45–60 SECONDS

NOTES/FOOD CHOICES

OVERALL RATING

POOR   ACCEPTABLE   GOOD   EXCELLENT   EXCEPTIONAL

TASTING NOTES

DATE   /   /

NAME

VINTAGE   COUNTRY/REGION

PRICE   GRAPES

COLOR   (P. 59)

AROMAS / BOUQUET   (P. 6–7)

FLAVORS   (P. 62)

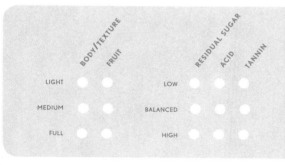

60-SECOND WINE TASTING

0–15 SECONDS

15–30 SECONDS

30–45 SECONDS

45–60 SECONDS

NOTES/FOOD CHOICES

OVERALL RATING

POOR   ACCEPTABLE   GOOD   EXCELLENT   EXCEPTIONAL

🍇 **TASTING NOTES**   DATE   /   /

NAME

VINTAGE   COUNTRY/REGION

PRICE   GRAPES

COLOR   (P. 59)

AROMAS / BOUQUET   (P. 6-7)

FLAVORS   (P. 62)

	BODY/TEXTURE	FRUIT		RESIDUAL SUGAR	ACID	TANNIN
LIGHT	○	○	LOW	○	○	○
MEDIUM	○	○	BALANCED	○	○	○
FULL	○	○	HIGH	○	○	○

60-SECOND WINE TASTING

0-15 SECONDS

15-30 SECONDS

30-45 SECONDS

45-60 SECONDS

NOTES/FOOD CHOICES

OVERALL RATING

POOR   ACCEPTABLE   GOOD   EXCELLENT   EXCEPTIONAL

TASTING NOTES   DATE   /   /

NAME

VINTAGE   COUNTRY/REGION

PRICE   GRAPES

COLOR   (P. 59)

AROMAS / BOUQUET   (P. 6-7)

FLAVORS   (P. 62)

	BODY/TEXTURE	FRUIT		RESIDUAL SUGAR	ACID	TANNIN
LIGHT	○	○	LOW	○	○	○
MEDIUM	○	○	BALANCED	○	○	○
FULL	○	○	HIGH	○	○	○

CHECKLIST

60-SECOND WINE TASTING

0-15 SECONDS

15-30 SECONDS

30-45 SECONDS

45-60 SECONDS

NOTES/FOOD CHOICES

OVERALL RATING

POOR   ACCEPTABLE   GOOD   EXCELLENT   EXCEPTIONAL

🍇 TASTING NOTES   DATE   /   /

NAME

VINTAGE   COUNTRY/REGION

PRICE   GRAPES

COLOR   (P. 59)

AROMAS / BOUQUET   (P. 6-7)

FLAVORS   (P. 62)

CHECKLIST

	BODY/TEXTURE	FRUIT		RESIDUAL SUGAR	ACID	TANNIN
LIGHT	○	○	LOW	○	○	○
MEDIUM	○	○	BALANCED	○	○	○
FULL	○	○	HIGH	○	○	○

60-SECOND WINE TASTING

0-15 SECONDS

15-30 SECONDS

30-45 SECONDS

45-60 SECONDS

NOTES/FOOD CHOICES

OVERALL RATING

POOR   ACCEPTABLE   GOOD   EXCELLENT   EXCEPTIONAL
 ○   ○   ○   ○   ○

TASTING NOTES   DATE   /   /

NAME ....

VINTAGE   COUNTRY/REGION ....

PRICE   GRAPES ....

COLOR .... (P. 59)

AROMAS / BOUQUET .... (P. 6-7)

FLAVORS .... (P. 62)

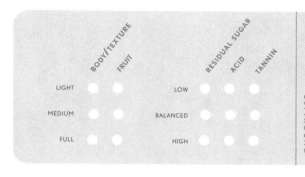

	BODY/TEXTURE	FRUIT		RESIDUAL SUGAR	ACID	TANNIN
LIGHT	○	○	LOW	○	○	○
MEDIUM	○	○	BALANCED	○	○	○
FULL	○	○	HIGH	○	○	○

CHECKLIST

60-SECOND WINE TASTING

0-15 SECONDS ....

15-30 SECONDS ....

30-45 SECONDS ....

45-60 SECONDS ....

NOTES/FOOD CHOICES
....
....

OVERALL RATING

POOR   ACCEPTABLE   GOOD   EXCELLENT   EXCEPTIONAL
○   ○   ○   ○   ○

TASTING NOTES

DATE ___ / ___ / ___

NAME _____

VINTAGE _____ COUNTRY/REGION _____

PRICE _____ GRAPES _____

COLOR _____ (P. 59)

AROMAS / BOUQUET _____ (P. 6-7)

FLAVORS _____ (P. 62)

CHECKLIST

	BODY/TEXTURE	FRUIT		RESIDUAL SUGAR	ACID	TANNIN
LIGHT	○	○	LOW	○	○	○
MEDIUM	○	○	BALANCED	○	○	○
FULL	○	○	HIGH	○	○	○

60-SECOND WINE TASTING

0–15 SECONDS _____

15–30 SECONDS _____

30–45 SECONDS _____

45–60 SECONDS _____

NOTES/FOOD CHOICES _____

_____

_____

OVERALL RATING

POOR   ACCEPTABLE   GOOD   EXCELLENT   EXCEPTIONAL
 ○   ○   ○   ○   ○

TASTING NOTES   DATE   /   /

NAME

VINTAGE   COUNTRY/REGION

PRICE   GRAPES

COLOR   (P. 59)

AROMAS / BOUQUET   (P. 6-7)

FLAVORS   (P. 62)

	BODY/TEXTURE	FRUIT		RESIDUAL SUGAR	ACID	TANNIN
LIGHT	○	○	LOW	○	○	○
MEDIUM	○	○	BALANCED	○	○	○
FULL	○	○	HIGH	○	○	○

CHECKLIST

60-SECOND WINE TASTING

0-15 SECONDS

15-30 SECONDS

30-45 SECONDS

45-60 SECONDS

NOTES/FOOD CHOICES

OVERALL RATING

POOR   ACCEPTABLE   GOOD   EXCELLENT   EXCEPTIONAL

🍇 TASTING NOTES

DATE   /   /

NAME

VINTAGE   COUNTRY/REGION

PRICE   GRAPES

COLOR   (P. 59)

AROMAS / BOUQUET   (P. 6–7)

FLAVORS   (P. 62)

CHECKLIST

	BODY/TEXTURE	FRUIT		RESIDUAL SUGAR	ACID	TANNIN
LIGHT	○	○	LOW	○	○	○
MEDIUM	○	○	BALANCED	○	○	○
FULL	○	○	HIGH	○	○	○

60-SECOND WINE TASTING

0–15 SECONDS

15–30 SECONDS

30–45 SECONDS

45–60 SECONDS

NOTES/FOOD CHOICES

OVERALL RATING

POOR   ACCEPTABLE   GOOD   EXCELLENT   EXCEPTIONAL

TASTING NOTES   DATE   /   /

NAME

VINTAGE   COUNTRY/REGION

PRICE   GRAPES

COLOR   (P. 59)

AROMAS / BOUQUET   (P. 6-7)

FLAVORS   (P. 62)

	BODY/TEXTURE	FRUIT		RESIDUAL SUGAR	ACID	TANNIN
LIGHT	○	○	LOW	○	○	○
MEDIUM	○	○	BALANCED	○	○	○
FULL	○	○	HIGH	○	○	○

CHECKLIST

60-SECOND WINE TASTING

0-15 SECONDS

15-30 SECONDS

30-45 SECONDS

45-60 SECONDS

NOTES/FOOD CHOICES

OVERALL RATING

POOR   ACCEPTABLE   GOOD   EXCELLENT   EXCEPTIONAL
 ○   ○   ○   ○   ○

TASTING NOTES

DATE   /   /

NAME

VINTAGE   COUNTRY/REGION

PRICE   GRAPES

COLOR   (P. 59)

AROMAS / BOUQUET   (P. 6-7)

FLAVORS   (P. 62)

CHECKLIST

	BODY/TEXTURE	FRUIT		RESIDUAL SUGAR	ACID	TANNIN
LIGHT	○	○	LOW	○	○	○
MEDIUM	○	○	BALANCED	○	○	○
FULL	○	○	HIGH	○	○	○

60-SECOND WINE TASTING

0-15 SECONDS

15-30 SECONDS

30-45 SECONDS

45-60 SECONDS

NOTES/FOOD CHOICES

OVERALL RATING

POOR	ACCEPTABLE	GOOD	EXCELLENT	EXCEPTIONAL
○	○	○	○	○

TASTING NOTES

DATE / /

NAME

VINTAGE   COUNTRY/REGION

PRICE   GRAPES

COLOR   (P. 59)

AROMAS / BOUQUET   (P. 6–7)

FLAVORS   (P. 62)

	BODY/TEXTURE	FRUIT		RESIDUAL SUGAR	ACID	TANNIN
LIGHT	○	○	LOW	○	○	○
MEDIUM	○	○	BALANCED	○	○	○
FULL	○	○	HIGH	○	○	○

CHECKLIST

60-SECOND WINE TASTING

0–15 SECONDS

15–30 SECONDS

30–45 SECONDS

45–60 SECONDS

NOTES/FOOD CHOICES

OVERALL RATING

POOR   ACCEPTABLE   GOOD   EXCELLENT   EXCEPTIONAL

🍇 TASTING NOTES   DATE   /   /

NAME _____

VINTAGE _____ COUNTRY/REGION _____

PRICE _____ GRAPES _____

COLOR _____ (P. 59)

AROMAS / BOUQUET _____ (P. 6–7)

FLAVORS _____ (P. 62)

CHECKLIST

	BODY/TEXTURE	FRUIT		RESIDUAL SUGAR	ACID	TANNIN
LIGHT	○	○	LOW	○	○	○
MEDIUM	○	○	BALANCED	○	○	○
FULL	○	○	HIGH	○	○	○

60-SECOND WINE TASTING

0–15 SECONDS _____

15–30 SECONDS _____

30–45 SECONDS _____

45–60 SECONDS _____

NOTES/FOOD CHOICES

_____

_____

OVERALL RATING

POOR   ACCEPTABLE   GOOD   EXCELLENT   EXCEPTIONAL
 ○   ○   ○   ○   ○

TASTING NOTES   DATE   /   /

NAME
....

VINTAGE   COUNTRY/REGION
....

PRICE   GRAPES
....

COLOR   (P. 59)
....

AROMAS / BOUQUET   (P. 6-7)
....

FLAVORS   (P. 62)
....

	BODY/TEXTURE	FRUIT		RESIDUAL SUGAR	ACID	TANNIN
LIGHT	○	○	LOW	○	○	○
MEDIUM	○	○	BALANCED	○	○	○
FULL	○	○	HIGH	○	○	○

CHECKLIST

60-SECOND WINE TASTING

0–15 SECONDS
....

15–30 SECONDS
....

30–45 SECONDS
....

45–60 SECONDS

NOTES/FOOD CHOICES
....
....

OVERALL RATING

POOR   ACCEPTABLE   GOOD   EXCELLENT   EXCEPTIONAL
 ○   ○   ○   ○   ○

TASTING NOTES

DATE   /   /

NAME

VINTAGE   COUNTRY/REGION

PRICE   GRAPES

COLOR   (P. 59)

AROMAS / BOUQUET   (P. 6-7)

FLAVORS   (P. 62)

	BODY/TEXTURE	FRUIT		RESIDUAL SUGAR	ACID	TANNIN
LIGHT	○	○	LOW	○	○	○
MEDIUM	○	○	BALANCED	○	○	○
FULL	○	○	HIGH	○	○	○

CHECKLIST

60-SECOND WINE TASTING

0-15 SECONDS

15-30 SECONDS

30-45 SECONDS

45-60 SECONDS

NOTES/FOOD CHOICES

OVERALL RATING

POOR   ACCEPTABLE   GOOD   EXCELLENT   EXCEPTIONAL

TASTING NOTES

DATE / /

NAME

VINTAGE   COUNTRY/REGION

PRICE   GRAPES

COLOR   (P. 59)

AROMAS / BOUQUET   (P. 6-7)

FLAVORS   (P. 62)

	BODY/TEXTURE	FRUIT		RESIDUAL SUGAR	ACID	TANNIN
LIGHT	◯	◯	LOW	◯	◯	◯
MEDIUM	◯	◯	BALANCED	◯	◯	◯
FULL	◯	◯	HIGH	◯	◯	◯

CHECKLIST

60-SECOND WINE TASTING

0-15 SECONDS

15-30 SECONDS

30-45 SECONDS

45-60 SECONDS

NOTES/FOOD CHOICES

OVERALL RATING

POOR   ACCEPTABLE   GOOD   EXCELLENT   EXCEPTIONAL
◯   ◯   ◯   ◯   ◯

🍇 TASTING NOTES   DATE / /

NAME

VINTAGE   COUNTRY/REGION

PRICE   GRAPES

COLOR   (P. 59)

AROMAS / BOUQUET   (P. 6-7)

FLAVORS   (P. 62)

CHECKLIST

	BODY/TEXTURE	FRUIT		RESIDUAL SUGAR	ACID	TANNIN
LIGHT	○	○	LOW	○	○	○
MEDIUM	○	○	BALANCED	○	○	○
FULL	○	○	HIGH	○	○	○

60-SECOND WINE TASTING

0-15 SECONDS

15-30 SECONDS

30-45 SECONDS

45-60 SECONDS

NOTES/FOOD CHOICES

OVERALL RATING

POOR ACCEPTABLE GOOD EXCELLENT EXCEPTIONAL

TASTING NOTES

DATE   /   /

NAME

VINTAGE   COUNTRY/REGION

PRICE   GRAPES

COLOR   (P. 59)

AROMAS / BOUQUET   (P. 6–7)

FLAVORS   (P. 62)

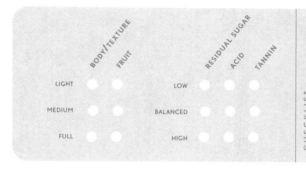

	BODY/TEXTURE	FRUIT			RESIDUAL SUGAR	ACID	TANNIN
LIGHT	○	○	LOW		○	○	○
MEDIUM	○	○	BALANCED		○	○	○
FULL	○	○	HIGH		○	○	○

CHECKLIST

60-SECOND WINE TASTING

0–15 SECONDS

15–30 SECONDS

30–45 SECONDS

45–60 SECONDS

NOTES/FOOD CHOICES

OVERALL RATING

POOR	ACCEPTABLE	GOOD	EXCELLENT	EXCEPTIONAL
○	○	○	○	○

TASTING NOTES

DATE   /   /

NAME

VINTAGE   COUNTRY/REGION

PRICE   GRAPES

COLOR   (P. 59)

AROMAS / BOUQUET   (P. 6-7)

FLAVORS   (P. 62)

CHECKLIST

	BODY/TEXTURE	FRUIT		RESIDUAL SUGAR	ACID	TANNIN
LIGHT	○	○	LOW	○	○	○
MEDIUM	○	○	BALANCED	○	○	○
FULL	○	○	HIGH	○	○	○

60-SECOND WINE TASTING

0-15 SECONDS

15-30 SECONDS

30-45 SECONDS

45-60 SECONDS

NOTES/FOOD CHOICES

OVERALL RATING

POOR	ACCEPTABLE	GOOD	EXCELLENT	EXCEPTIONAL
●	●	●	●	●

TASTING NOTES   DATE   /   /

NAME

VINTAGE   COUNTRY/REGION

PRICE   GRAPES

COLOR   (P. 59)

AROMAS / BOUQUET   (P. 6–7)

FLAVORS   (P. 62)

	BODY/TEXTURE	FRUIT		RESIDUAL SUGAR	ACID	TANNIN
LIGHT	○	○	LOW	○	○	○
MEDIUM	○	○	BALANCED	○	○	○
FULL	○	○	HIGH	○	○	○

CHECKLIST

60-SECOND WINE TASTING

0–15 SECONDS

15–30 SECONDS

30–45 SECONDS

45–60 SECONDS

NOTES/FOOD CHOICES

OVERALL RATING

POOR   ACCEPTABLE   GOOD   EXCELLENT   EXCEPTIONAL
 ○   ○   ○   ○   ○

🍇 TASTING NOTES   DATE   /   /

NAME

VINTAGE   COUNTRY/REGION

PRICE   GRAPES

COLOR   (P. 59)

AROMAS / BOUQUET   (P. 6-7)

FLAVORS   (P. 62)

CHECKLIST

	BODY/TEXTURE	FRUIT		RESIDUAL SUGAR	ACID	TANNIN
LIGHT	○	○	LOW	○	○	○
MEDIUM	○	○	BALANCED	○	○	○
FULL	○	○	HIGH	○	○	○

60-SECOND WINE TASTING

0-15 SECONDS

15-30 SECONDS

30-45 SECONDS

45-60 SECONDS

NOTES/FOOD CHOICES

OVERALL RATING

POOR   ACCEPTABLE   GOOD   EXCELLENT   EXCEPTIONAL
 ○   ○   ○   ○   ○

TASTING NOTES

DATE / /

NAME ....

VINTAGE .... COUNTRY/REGION ....

PRICE .... GRAPES ....

COLOR .... (P. 59)

AROMAS / BOUQUET .... (P. 6-7)

FLAVORS .... (P. 62)

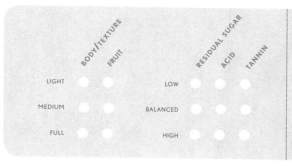

BODY/TEXTURE FRUIT RESIDUAL SUGAR ACID TANNIN

LIGHT ● ● LOW ● ● ●

MEDIUM ● ● BALANCED ● ● ●

FULL ● ● HIGH ● ● ●

CHECKLIST

60-SECOND WINE TASTING

0-15 SECONDS ....

15-30 SECONDS ....

30-45 SECONDS ....

45-60 SECONDS ....

NOTES/FOOD CHOICES
....
....

OVERALL RATING

POOR   ACCEPTABLE   GOOD   EXCELLENT   EXCEPTIONAL

TASTING NOTES

DATE / /

NAME

VINTAGE   COUNTRY/REGION

PRICE   GRAPES

COLOR   (P. 59)

AROMAS / BOUQUET   (P. 6-7)

FLAVORS   (P. 62)

CHECKLIST

	BODY/TEXTURE	FRUIT		RESIDUAL SUGAR	ACID	TANNIN
LIGHT	○	○	LOW	○	○	○
MEDIUM	○	○	BALANCED	○	○	○
FULL	○	○	HIGH	○	○	○

60-SECOND WINE TASTING

0-15 SECONDS

15-30 SECONDS

30-45 SECONDS

45-60 SECONDS

NOTES/FOOD CHOICES

OVERALL RATING

POOR   ACCEPTABLE   GOOD   EXCELLENT   EXCEPTIONAL

TASTING NOTES   DATE   /   /

NAME

VINTAGE   COUNTRY/REGION

PRICE   GRAPES

COLOR   (P. 59)

AROMAS / BOUQUET   (P. 6-7)

FLAVORS   (P. 62)

	BODY/TEXTURE	FRUIT		RESIDUAL SUGAR	ACID	TANNIN
LIGHT	○	○	LOW	○	○	○
MEDIUM	○	○	BALANCED	○	○	○
FULL	○	○	HIGH	○	○	○

CHECKLIST

60-SECOND WINE TASTING

0-15 SECONDS

15-30 SECONDS

30-45 SECONDS

45-60 SECONDS

NOTES/FOOD CHOICES

OVERALL RATING

POOR   ACCEPTABLE   GOOD   EXCELLENT   EXCEPTIONAL
 ○   ○   ○   ○   ○

🍇 TASTING NOTES

DATE   /   /

NAME

VINTAGE   COUNTRY/REGION

PRICE   GRAPES

COLOR   (P. 59)

AROMAS / BOUQUET   (P. 6-7)

FLAVORS   (P. 62)

CHECKLIST

	BODY/TEXTURE	FRUIT		RESIDUAL SUGAR	ACID	TANNIN
LIGHT	○	○	LOW	○	○	○
MEDIUM	○	○	BALANCED	○	○	○
FULL	○	○	HIGH	○	○	○

60-SECOND WINE TASTING

0-15 SECONDS

15-30 SECONDS

30-45 SECONDS

45-60 SECONDS

NOTES/FOOD CHOICES

OVERALL RATING

POOR   ACCEPTABLE   GOOD   EXCELLENT   EXCEPTIONAL

TASTING NOTES   DATE   /   /

NAME

VINTAGE   COUNTRY/REGION

PRICE   GRAPES

COLOR   (P. 59)

AROMAS / BOUQUET   (P. 6–7)

FLAVORS   (P. 62)

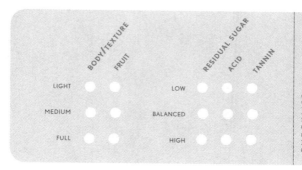

60-SECOND WINE TASTING

0–15 SECONDS

15–30 SECONDS

30–45 SECONDS

45–60 SECONDS

NOTES/FOOD CHOICES

OVERALL RATING

POOR   ACCEPTABLE   GOOD   EXCELLENT   EXCEPTIONAL

🍇 TASTING NOTES

DATE   /   /

NAME

VINTAGE   COUNTRY/REGION

PRICE   GRAPES

COLOR   (P. 59)

AROMAS / BOUQUET   (P. 6–7)

FLAVORS   (P. 62)

CHECKLIST

BODY/TEXTURE   FRUIT   RESIDUAL SUGAR   ACID   TANNIN

LIGHT   ○   ○   LOW   ○   ○   ○

MEDIUM   ○   ○   BALANCED   ○   ○   ○

FULL   ○   ○   HIGH   ○   ○   ○

60-SECOND WINE TASTING

0–15 SECONDS

15–30 SECONDS

30–45 SECONDS

45–60 SECONDS

NOTES/FOOD CHOICES

OVERALL RATING

POOR   ACCEPTABLE   GOOD   EXCELLENT   EXCEPTIONAL
●   ●   ●   ●   ●

NAME

VINTAGE COUNTRY/REGION

PRICE GRAPES

COLOR (P. 59)

AROMAS / BOUQUET (P. 6-7)

FLAVORS (P. 62)

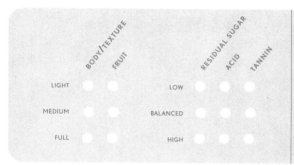

	BODY/TEXTURE	FRUIT		RESIDUAL SUGAR	ACID	TANNIN
LIGHT	○	○	LOW	○	○	○
MEDIUM	○	○	BALANCED	○	○	○
FULL	○	○	HIGH	○	○	○

CHECKLIST

60-SECOND WINE TASTING

0-15 SECONDS

15-30 SECONDS

30-45 SECONDS

45-60 SECONDS

NOTES/FOOD CHOICES

OVERALL RATING

POOR   ACCEPTABLE   GOOD   EXCELLENT   EXCEPTIONAL

TASTING NOTES   DATE   /   /

NAME

VINTAGE   COUNTRY/REGION

PRICE   GRAPES

COLOR   (P. 59)

AROMAS / BOUQUET   (P. 6-7)

FLAVORS   (P. 62)

CHECKLIST

	BODY/TEXTURE	FRUIT		RESIDUAL SUGAR	ACID	TANNIN
LIGHT	○	○	LOW	○	○	○
MEDIUM	○	○	BALANCED	○	○	○
FULL	○	○	HIGH	○	○	○

60-SECOND WINE TASTING

0-15 SECONDS

15-30 SECONDS

30-45 SECONDS

45-60 SECONDS

NOTES/FOOD CHOICES

OVERALL RATING

POOR   ACCEPTABLE   GOOD   EXCELLENT   EXCEPTIONAL

TASTING NOTES   DATE   /   /

NAME

VINTAGE   COUNTRY/REGION

PRICE   GRAPES

COLOR   (P. 59)

AROMAS / BOUQUET   (P. 6-7)

FLAVORS   (P. 62)

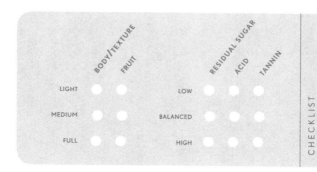

60-SECOND WINE TASTING

0-15 SECONDS

15-30 SECONDS

30-45 SECONDS

45-60 SECONDS

NOTES/FOOD CHOICES

OVERALL RATING

POOR   ACCEPTABLE   GOOD   EXCELLENT   EXCEPTIONAL

TASTING NOTES

DATE / /

NAME

VINTAGE COUNTRY/REGION

PRICE GRAPES

COLOR (P. 59)

AROMAS / BOUQUET (P. 6-7)

FLAVORS (P. 62)

CHECKLIST

	BODY/TEXTURE	FRUIT		RESIDUAL SUGAR	ACID	TANNIN
LIGHT	◯	◯	LOW	◯	◯	◯
MEDIUM	◯	◯	BALANCED	◯	◯	◯
FULL	◯	◯	HIGH	◯	◯	◯

60-SECOND WINE TASTING

0-15 SECONDS

15-30 SECONDS

30-45 SECONDS

45-60 SECONDS

NOTES/FOOD CHOICES

OVERALL RATING

POOR   ACCEPTABLE   GOOD   EXCELLENT   EXCEPTIONAL

TASTING NOTES   DATE   /   /

NAME
....

VINTAGE   COUNTRY/REGION
....

PRICE   GRAPES
....

COLOR   (P. 59)
....

AROMAS / BOUQUET   (P. 6-7)
....

FLAVORS   (P. 62)
....

	BODY/TEXTURE	FRUIT		RESIDUAL SUGAR	ACID	TANNIN
LIGHT	○	○	LOW	○	○	○
MEDIUM	○	○	BALANCED	○	○	○
FULL	○	○	HIGH	○	○	○

CHECKLIST

60-SECOND WINE TASTING

0-15 SECONDS
....

15-30 SECONDS
....

30-45 SECONDS
....

45-60 SECONDS
....

NOTES/FOOD CHOICES
....
....

OVERALL RATING

POOR   ACCEPTABLE   GOOD   EXCELLENT   EXCEPTIONAL
 ○   ○   ○   ○   ○

🍇 TASTING NOTES

DATE   /   /

NAME

VINTAGE   COUNTRY/REGION

PRICE   GRAPES

COLOR   (P. 59)

AROMAS / BOUQUET   (P. 6-7)

FLAVORS   (P. 62)

(P. 59) (P. 6-7) (P. 62)

CHECKLIST

	BODY/TEXTURE	FRUIT		RESIDUAL SUGAR	ACID	TANNIN
LIGHT	○	○	LOW	○	○	○
MEDIUM	○	○	BALANCED	○	○	○
FULL	○	○	HIGH	○	○	○

60-SECOND WINE TASTING

0-15 SECONDS

15-30 SECONDS

30-45 SECONDS

45-60 SECONDS

NOTES/FOOD CHOICES

OVERALL RATING

POOR   ACCEPTABLE   GOOD   EXCELLENT   EXCEPTIONAL

TASTING NOTES

DATE   /   /

NAME

VINTAGE   COUNTRY/REGION

PRICE   GRAPES

COLOR   (P. 59)

AROMAS / BOUQUET   (P. 6-7)

FLAVORS   (P. 62)

	BODY/TEXTURE	FRUIT		RESIDUAL SUGAR	ACID	TANNIN
LIGHT	○	○	LOW	○	○	○
MEDIUM	○	○	BALANCED	○	○	○
FULL	○	○	HIGH	○	○	○

CHECKLIST

60-SECOND WINE TASTING

0-15 SECONDS

15-30 SECONDS

30-45 SECONDS

45-60 SECONDS

NOTES/FOOD CHOICES

OVERALL RATING

POOR   ACCEPTABLE   GOOD   EXCELLENT   EXCEPTIONAL
 ○   ○   ○   ○   ○

TASTING NOTES   DATE   /   /

NAME

VINTAGE   COUNTRY/REGION

PRICE   GRAPES

COLOR   (P. 59)

AROMAS / BOUQUET   (P. 6-7)

FLAVORS   (P. 62)

CHECKLIST		BODY/TEXTURE	FRUIT			RESIDUAL SUGAR	ACID	TANNIN
	LIGHT	○	○	LOW		○	○	○
	MEDIUM	○	○	BALANCED		○	○	○
	FULL	○	○	HIGH		○	○	○

60-SECOND WINE TASTING

0–15 SECONDS

15–30 SECONDS

30–45 SECONDS

45–60 SECONDS

NOTES/FOOD CHOICES

OVERALL RATING

POOR   ACCEPTABLE   GOOD   EXCELLENT   EXCEPTIONAL
 ○   ○   ○   ○   ○

TASTING NOTES DATE   /   /

NAME

VINTAGE   COUNTRY/REGION

PRICE   GRAPES

COLOR   (P. 59)

AROMAS / BOUQUET   (P. 6-7)

FLAVORS   (P. 62)

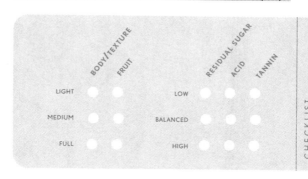

60-SECOND WINE TASTING

0-15 SECONDS

15-30 SECONDS

30-45 SECONDS

45-60 SECONDS

NOTES/FOOD CHOICES

OVERALL RATING

POOR   ACCEPTABLE   GOOD   EXCELLENT   EXCEPTIONAL

TASTING NOTES   DATE   /   /

NAME

VINTAGE   COUNTRY/REGION

PRICE   GRAPES

COLOR   (P. 59)

AROMAS / BOUQUET   (P. 6-7)

FLAVORS   (P. 62)

CHECKLIST		BODY/TEXTURE	FRUIT			RESIDUAL SUGAR	ACID	TANNIN
	LIGHT	○	○	LOW		○	○	○
	MEDIUM	○	○	BALANCED		○	○	○
	FULL	○	○	HIGH		○	○	○

60-SECOND WINE TASTING

0-15 SECONDS

15-30 SECONDS

30-45 SECONDS

45-60 SECONDS

NOTES/FOOD CHOICES

OVERALL RATING

POOR   ACCEPTABLE   GOOD   EXCELLENT   EXCEPTIONAL
 ○   ○   ○   ○   ○

TASTING NOTES   DATE   /   /

NAME ....

VINTAGE   COUNTRY/REGION ....

PRICE   GRAPES ....

COLOR ....   (P. 59)

AROMAS / BOUQUET ....   (P. 6–7)

FLAVORS ....   (P. 62)

	BODY/TEXTURE	FRUIT		RESIDUAL SUGAR	ACID	TANNIN
LIGHT	○	○	LOW	○	○	○
MEDIUM	○	○	BALANCED	○	○	○
FULL	○	○	HIGH	○	○	○

CHECKLIST

60-SECOND WINE TASTING

0–15 SECONDS ....

15–30 SECONDS ....

30–45 SECONDS ....

45–60 SECONDS ....

NOTES/FOOD CHOICES

....

....

OVERALL RATING

POOR   ACCEPTABLE   GOOD   EXCELLENT   EXCEPTIONAL
○   ○   ○   ○   ○

TASTING NOTES

DATE   /   /

NAME

VINTAGE   COUNTRY/REGION

PRICE   GRAPES

COLOR   (P. 59)

AROMAS / BOUQUET   (P. 6-7)

FLAVORS   (P. 62)

(P. 59)
(P. 6-7)
(P. 62)

CHECKLIST

	BODY/TEXTURE	FRUIT			RESIDUAL SUGAR	ACID	TANNIN
LIGHT	○	○	LOW		○	○	○
MEDIUM	○	○	BALANCED		○	○	○
FULL	○	○	HIGH		○	○	○

60-SECOND WINE TASTING

0-15 SECONDS

15-30 SECONDS

30-45 SECONDS

45-60 SECONDS

NOTES/FOOD CHOICES

OVERALL RATING

POOR   ACCEPTABLE   GOOD   EXCELLENT   EXCEPTIONAL

TASTING NOTES DATE / /

NAME

VINTAGE   COUNTRY/REGION

PRICE   GRAPES

COLOR   (P. 59)

AROMAS / BOUQUET   (P. 6–7)

FLAVORS   (P. 62)

	BODY/TEXTURE	FRUIT		RESIDUAL SUGAR	ACID	TANNIN
LIGHT	○	○	LOW	○	○	○
MEDIUM	○	○	BALANCED	○	○	○
FULL	○	○	HIGH	○	○	○

CHECKLIST

60-SECOND WINE TASTING

0–15 SECONDS

15–30 SECONDS

30–45 SECONDS

45–60 SECONDS

NOTES/FOOD CHOICES

OVERALL RATING

POOR   ACCEPTABLE   GOOD   EXCELLENT   EXCEPTIONAL
 ○   ○   ○   ○   ○

TASTING NOTES

DATE   /   /

NAME ....

VINTAGE .... COUNTRY/REGION ....

PRICE .... GRAPES ....

COLOR .... (P. 59)

AROMAS / BOUQUET .... (P. 6-7)

FLAVORS .... (P. 62)

CHECKLIST

	BODY/TEXTURE	FRUIT		RESIDUAL SUGAR	ACID	TANNIN
LIGHT	○	○	LOW	○	○	○
MEDIUM	○	○	BALANCED	○	○	○
FULL	○	○	HIGH	○	○	○

60-SECOND WINE TASTING

0-15 SECONDS ....

15-30 SECONDS ....

30-45 SECONDS ....

45-60 SECONDS ....

NOTES/FOOD CHOICES

....

....

OVERALL RATING

POOR   ACCEPTABLE   GOOD   EXCELLENT   EXCEPTIONAL
○   ○   ○   ○   ○

TASTING NOTES

DATE   /   /

NAME ....

VINTAGE .... COUNTRY/REGION ....

PRICE .... GRAPES ....

COLOR .... (P. 59)

AROMAS / BOUQUET .... (P. 6–7)

FLAVORS .... (P. 62)

	BODY/TEXTURE	FRUIT		RESIDUAL SUGAR	ACID	TANNIN
LIGHT	○	○	LOW	○	○	○
MEDIUM	○	○	BALANCED	○	○	○
FULL	○	○	HIGH	○	○	○

CHECKLIST

60-SECOND WINE TASTING

0–15 SECONDS ....

15–30 SECONDS ....

30–45 SECONDS ....

45–60 SECONDS ....

NOTES/FOOD CHOICES

....

....

OVERALL RATING

POOR   ACCEPTABLE   GOOD   EXCELLENT   EXCEPTIONAL

  ○   ○   ○   ○   ○

TASTING NOTES   DATE   /   /

NAME ....

VINTAGE .... COUNTRY/REGION ....

PRICE .... GRAPES ....

COLOR .... (P. 59)

AROMAS / BOUQUET .... (P. 6-7)

FLAVORS .... (P. 62)

CHECKLIST

BODY/TEXTURE FRUIT   RESIDUAL SUGAR ACID TANNIN

LIGHT   ○   ○   LOW   ○   ○   ○

MEDIUM   ○   ○   BALANCED   ○   ○   ○

FULL   ○   ○   HIGH   ○   ○   ○

60-SECOND WINE TASTING

0-15 SECONDS ....

15-30 SECONDS ....

30-45 SECONDS ....

45-60 SECONDS ....

NOTES/FOOD CHOICES

....

....

OVERALL RATING

POOR   ACCEPTABLE   GOOD   EXCELLENT   EXCEPTIONAL
 ○   ○   ○   ○   ○

TASTING NOTES

DATE / /

NAME

VINTAGE   COUNTRY/REGION

PRICE   GRAPES

COLOR   (P. 59)

AROMAS / BOUQUET   (P. 6-7)

FLAVORS   (P. 62)

	BODY/TEXTURE	FRUIT		RESIDUAL SUGAR	ACID	TANNIN
LIGHT	○	○	LOW	○	○	○
MEDIUM	○	○	BALANCED	○	○	○
FULL	○	○	HIGH	○	○	○

CHECKLIST

60-SECOND WINE TASTING

0-15 SECONDS

15-30 SECONDS

30-45 SECONDS

45-60 SECONDS

NOTES/FOOD CHOICES

OVERALL RATING

POOR   ACCEPTABLE   GOOD   EXCELLENT   EXCEPTIONAL
○   ○   ○   ○   ○

ABOUT THE AUTHOR

KEVIN ZRALY is the founder and teacher of the Windows on the World Wine School, now in its 39th year, which has graduated more than 20,000 students. Author of the *Windows on the World Complete Wine Course* (Sterling Epicure), which has sold more than 3 million copies, he is the world's bestselling wine author and has received the James Beard Lifetime Achievement Award and the European Wine Council's Lifetime Achievement Award, among numerous others. He has been featured in GQ, *The New York Times, Newsweek, People, USA Today, Wall Street Journal,* and other publications.